LIKE A DREAM, LIKE A FANTASY

PUBLISHER'S ACKNOWLEDGMENT

The publisher gratefully acknowledges the generous help of the Hershey Family Foundation in sponsoring the printing of this book.

LIKE A DREAM
LIKE A FANTASY

*The Zen Teachings and Translations
of Nyogen Senzaki*

Edited and Introduced by Eidō Shimano
Preface by Sōen Nakagawa

Wisdom Publications • Boston

Wisdom Publications, Inc.
199 Elm Street
Somerville MA 02144 USA
www.wisdompubs.org

Library of Congress Cataloging-in-Publication Data
Senzaki, Nyogen.
  Like a dream, like a fantasy : the Zen teachings and translations of Nyogen Senzaki / edited and introduced by Eido Shimano ; preface by Soen Nakagawa ; [author[s] Senzaki Nyogen, Shimano Eido].
    p. cm.
  Pieces in item represent Senzaki's writings and talks, as well as his translations and original poetry.
  Includes bibliographical references and index.
  ISBN 0-86171-280-3 (pbk. : alk. paper)
  1. Zen Buddhism. 2. Religious life—Zen Buddhism. I. Shimano, Eido, 1932-
II. Title.
  BQ9266. S46 2005
  294.3'420427—dc22
                              2005016788

ISBN 0-86171-280-3

First Wisdom edition
09 08 07 06 05
5   4   3   2   1

Cover design by Rick Snizik.
Interior design by Gopa &Ted2, Inc. Set in Diacritical Garamond 11/16 pt.

Wisdom Publications' books are printed on acid-free paper and meet the guidelines for permanence and durability set by the Council of Library Resources.

Printed in the United States of America.

CONTENTS

The Zen Teachings and Translations of Nyogen Senzaki

一人つゝ来て是月さす窓ちかく
今宵うす茶を公案にして

LETTER TO
NYOGEN SENZAKI

Letter to Nyogen Senzaki

Note: The following letter was written by Sōen Nakagawa Rōshi, Abbot of Ryūtaku-ji, to his dear friend Nyogen Senzaki just after hearing of Senzaki's passing. Sōen Rōshi and Senzaki Sensei had been corresponding with each other ever since 1934, when the latter read some of young monk Sōen's poems and essays published in a Japanese magazine, Fujin Koron. Because of World War II, the two men were unable to meet face to face until 1949, when Sōen Rōshi made his first trip to the United States. Eidō Shimano Rōshi, Sōen Rōshi's Dharma heir, wrote of this in Endless Vow: The Zen Path of Sōen Nakagawa: *"Their first-time meeting was truly an unprecedented and unrepeatable manifestation of a rare and beautiful friendship." They were able to see each other again in California in 1955, and the following year Senzaki Sensei returned to Japan for the first time in his nearly fifty years abroad. It was then, at Ryūtaku-ji, that Eidō Shimano met Nyogen Senzaki. "Yet through our brief encounter, our karmic connection became apparent," Eidō Rōshi writes in* Endless Vow. *"Sōen Rōshi arranged for me to become the Venerable Nyogen's attendant in America, but in 1958, before I could make the trip, we received news of Nyogen Senzaki's death."*

May 8, 1958

Dear Senzaki Sensei,

This morning as usual we woke up at 3:30 A.M. After morning service in
the Dharma Hall, there were two dawn sittings. During the first sitting,
I was in the zendo with the monks. Then the attendant monk hurried up
to me and informed me of a telephone call from Los Angeles. At that very
moment, as though struck by a bolt of lightning, my mind was joined by
yours. I heard Sister Shūbin [Tanahashi's] lamenting voice; Brother
Baioh's clear "okay!" The faces of McCanenny-san and Seiko-san seemed
visible to me.

> I am joining
> In your meeting
> With one mind!
> *[written in English]*

During the second sitting I called the monks to dokusan. The first one
who came in was a young novice monk (nineteen years old) who joined
the monastery early this April from the countryside of Shikoku Island.
Although he just started zazen very recently, he has been getting into
samādhi quickly and deeply. Completely filled with samādhi joy, he told
me that though he hadn't slept for the past four nights and days, he felt
as clear as ever.

What about before your birth?

What about after death?

Even these questions he answered clearly, one by one. Indeed, this must be the working of his karma, not only in this lifetime, but life after life.

The fourth person to come in was Monk Eidō [Shimano], and his kōan happened to be Tosotsu's "Three Barriers":

If you realize your true nature, you are free from life and death. When your eyes are closed, how can you be free from life and death? If you are free from life and death, you will know where you are going. When the four elements are disintegrated, where will you go?

On this occasion, at this time, we thoroughly examined and clarified this particular kōan, as I believe this is the best way to express our gratitude to you.

After finishing dokusan, I went up to [Yamamoto] Gempō Rōshi's quarters and informed him of your departure. He was lying on his bed but said, "He was a reincarnate, and will work even harder for the Dharma now that he is without hindrances."

I completely agree with him. *Nyogen, Nyohō* ["Like a Phantasm," "Like Dharma"], please guide us on our path and in our practice with all your might. Please give us your encouragement in our pursuit of Buddha's incomparable Way.

At 6:00 A.M., we took our breakfast. When you visited here in 1955 you sat at this very place and we ate rice with adzuki beans to toast your safe return to the United States. Just as we did that time, with some twenty monks and serious lay students, we are dedicating ourselves to the Buddha's Way. Please rest assured.

After breakfast, I announced your departure to all the monks and lay students. Three of us, Manuel C. from France, Monk Eidō, and I, offered incense and flowers (from my mother's hut) and we listened to the lecture you had given at the Tuesday talk at the Los Angeles Zendo on September 19, 1952, which had been recorded by Sister Seiko. I was deeply moved by what you said about the Way of Renunciation.

Today I will go to Koyama Zenkai (a group of lepers who meet for Zen practice). After the evening *han* we will hold a memorial service for you, chanting "The Great Compassionate Dhāraṇī," and we will listen to your recorded voice ("Searching for the Treasure"). As I think more about our unthinkable karmic encounter during this lifetime, many scenes and images flow through my mind like a picture scroll. I was getting ready to send cherry blossoms to your bedside for comfort, but as usual, being a poor letter-writer, it turned out to be too late. However, now I feel it was all right. This Matter is beyond correspondence and beyond words and letters, and I have even come to think that in the final analysis, Mind alone is good enough.

Last night I was in Mishima for the Zen meeting (held every seventh day of the month). I asked my friend Mrs. Meio, who will soon perform the Noh dance "Tomoe," to sing a passage from it.

> Falling petals know it is fundamentally empty
> Flowing water knows it has no fixed mind
> Mind clears all by itself....

After that was over, I gave a talk on "Karma and Fundamental Emptiness." I assume your departure may have taken place just around that time (Japanese time, 9:00 P.M. May 7; Los Angeles time, 5:00 A.M. May 7).

Dōkoku no
Hatete arikeri
Satsuki Fuji.

Cries of grief have ebbed
Here it stands
Mt. Fuji in May

Sōen
Nine bows

一人つゝ来ては月さす窓ちかく
今宵うす茶を公案にして

INTRODUCTION

Nyogen Senzaki after his ordination in 1901

WE ALL HAVE AT LEAST two or three unforgettable days in our lives, some event that becomes a turning point. For me, one such day was in October 1955, when I first met Nyogen Senzaki, at Ryūtaku-Ji in Japan. After staying in the United States for nearly half a century, Nyogen Senzaki had come back to Japan and was visiting Ryūtaku-Ji at the invitation of my teacher, Sōen Nakagawa Rōshi.

On that occasion Nyogen Senzaki told a story to the monks. Later he wrote it down:

MOONLIGHT PARTY

Every year on the full moon night in August, we have a meeting to commemorate Abe no Nakamaro (698–770), a Japanese youth who, for the first time in the history of Japan, went to study in China (in the year 716). His genius as a poet was recognized by the Emperor of China, and he was asked to stay, serving the royal family as a tutor. He stayed there thirty-four years, in this high and honorable position, associating with the men of letters of the era. He was a man of unselfish character. Even though he left Japan when he was only sixteen years old, he still could not forget his mother country.

The Emperor was very much moved by his request to return and gave Nakamaro his consent with warm sympathy. Nakamaro gave away everything he had among his friends—even a sword he liked so much he carried it with him day and night. He took off his gorgeous robe and put on the plain blue attire of the student. To him, life in China had been only a dream now past; he was returning to the land of cherry blossoms with an empty hand and a pining soul. His friends saw him off at the seashore of Ming State; the beautiful moon rose above the vastness of the sea, casting its silvery light on the endless waves. He could not help expressing his feeling in native verse—even though he had not spoken his mother tongue in thirty-four years. The *uta* (another name for a *waka,* a thirty-one syllable Japanese poem, sometimes expressed in song) he composed would read in English:

> Moon! Moon!
> I see you now above the vast field of blue waves.
> So, you are the same moon
> I looked at in my hometown of Kasuga,
> Rising above Mikasa Mountain.
> Though I have been getting older in this foreign land,
> You still have the same beautiful face.

This poem remains in the memory of the people of Mikado's land, and will perhaps be remembered by them forever. Nakamaro's ship ran into a terrible storm that forced him back to China, where he remained for the rest of his life, without ever returning to his longed-for country of moonlight.

Nyogen Senzaki spoke of the similarities between that story and his own decades-long separation from Japan, expressing how grateful he felt to be able to return at least once to his motherland. The way he conveyed his genuine gratitude was really impressive and moving.

Nyogen Senzaki's visit to Ryūtaku-Ji was short. But after he returned to the United States, Sōen Rōshi asked me to go to America to assist Senzaki. Though this never came to pass, on that day the first seed of my coming to the West was planted, and my dream-like connection with

Nyogen Senzaki began. After he passed away on May 7th, 1958, our relationship became deeper and deeper, continuing so to this day.

According to the record of the Town Hall of Fukaura, Aomori Prefecture, Japan, Nyogen Senzaki was born on October 5th, 1876, and was named Aizō Senzaki. However, he admitted to not really knowing his birthday. The only known fact about his early life is that his grandfather was a Pure Land Buddhist priest and that from the age of five Nyogen Senzaki was educated at his grandfather's temple, Sōkō-Ji. He was later ordained in a nearby Sōtō Zen temple in Fukaura on April 8th, 1895, and was given the name Nyogen ("Like a Fantasy").

For some mysterious reason, he then went to Engaku-Ji in Kamakura, one of the headquarters of the Rinzai School, and became a disciple of Sōyen Shaku Rōshi. Nyogen Senzaki's admiration for his teacher was unusually strong; the poems he dedicated to Sōyen Shaku Rōshi speak more eloquently than anything I could say. Without this Dharma connection, he probably wouldn't have been able to come to the United States in 1905. At Engaku-Ji, Nyogen Senzaki trained with someone of great influence in the transmission of Zen Buddhism to the West: the scholar and lay Zen student D.T. Suzuki.

Senzaki wrote a short essay on Sōyen Shaku Rōshi and D.T. Suzuki in 1951:

> The writings of Dr. D.T. Suzuki are largely responsible for people in the West first becoming familiar with the thought and culture of Asia and the meaning of the word Zen. As early as 1893, Sōyen Shaku Rōshi first came to the United States as a representative Japanese Buddhist sent to the World Parliament of Religions held in Chicago that year. Among the many friends he made in the United States was Dr. Paul Carus, who later invited D.T. Suzuki, a lay student of Sōyen Shaku, to help him edit his monthly magazine as well as to assist him with other translations.
>
> Sōyen Shaku came again to America in 1905 and stayed in a

Sōyen Shaku

private home while he taught some of the fundamentals of Zen. His sermons and lectures of the time were translated by D.T. Suzuki into English and published in book form by the Open Court Publishing Company, Chicago 1906, under the title *Sermons of a Zen Buddhist Monk.*

After twenty years in America, D.T. Suzuki returned to Japan and later, while teaching at Otani University, edited and wrote for the *Eastern Buddhist,* a magazine issued from that University. His writings, especially *Zen for Americans,* have been recognized by scholars of Europe and America, and have had a far-reaching effect on the thought of the West.

Sōyen Shaku passed from this world in Japan, November 1, 1919, leaving many disciples, followers, and more than forty books he had written in Japanese and Chinese. The influence of this pioneer teacher on American Zen should be understood by and well introduced to English-speaking people.

Upon leaving Engaku-Ji, Nyogen Senzaki returned to Aomori, but didn't become an ordinary temple priest. Instead, he established what he called the Mentorgarten or Butsu-Myō-Gaku-En (Buddhist-Seedlings-School-Garden), a kind of Buddhist kindergarten. He acted as principal, teacher, and even janitor. The following letter to Sōyen Shaku is the only document that speaks about this period of his life.

Your disciple lost his mother at the age of five. Because of complicated circumstances in my family, I was sent to my grandfather's place, where I stayed over ten years. My grandfather was a Buddhist priest of the Pure Land School. He was respected for his virtuous deeds and deep faith in Buddha's teaching. I was influenced by him, and my gratitude toward Buddha's compassion increased. In my fantasy I felt as if I were dwelling always in the Pure Land. Prostrations and confession became my highest joy. When I was sixteen years old, my grandfather passed away. Just before his departure he told me, "Even though you may want to renounce everything and become a monk, the Buddhist priests around this area and elsewhere as well are not real Buddhists. Don't join this pack of wolves." Your disciple completed the usual academic studies and went back to his father's place and decided to become a medical doctor. While preparing for the entrance examination, I frequently thought about how in my childhood I had been fed by the offerings of the faithful congregants. Unless I requited this in some way, I feared that I would reap bad karma. After my stepbrother was old enough, I relinquished my right to succeed the Senzaki property, and I determined to engage in social work for the rest of my life. My grandfather had left some funds for me to continue my studies.

When I was in Junior High School I read the autobiography of Benjamin Franklin. Every night, he engaged in introspection, writing down his deeds and marking the negative actions with a black dot. I imitated him and found that my notebook became full of black dots. I was depressed and disappointed in myself. I was also disappointed in the easy practice of the Pure Land School. I lost my confidence, and with a shaky state of mind, I studied Christianity for a short while. However, someone introduced me to the life of the haiku poet Bashō, through which I discovered Zen. I then started my own Zen practice and began invoking Amitābha Buddha's name. One day I read about the incident in which Zen Master Tokusan burned all his books. I suddenly decided to become a monk and was ordained at a Sōtō Zen temple (since here in Aomori there are only Sōtō School temples). Thus I shaved my head and became a Zen Buddhist monk....

After I left Engaku-Ji I came back to Fukaura, Aomori prefecture. There are four Buddhist temples here. What the priests do is nothing but funerals and some other rituals, but there is no practice. Whenever there is some gathering among the priests of those temples, they drink sakē, bring instruments, and chant folk songs. The education level is extremely low. Teachers are reluctant to live in Fukaura. As a result, the children receive a very poor education. Your disciple, though he is aware of his stupidity and lack of virtue, can't help but try to save others before himself. I decided to start a school to educate children. Do you think that my passion may become a real fire and that this would be an effective way to be a Buddhist monk? I feel that if I approach young children, they will gather around me, and I can teach Buddha's way as well as the necessary subjects. I would really like to do this, but I feel that the final decision should be made by my beloved teacher and I will await your decision....

After my ordination, I never touched the offerings made to the temple. However, I may have to change my attitude in order to spread the Dharma the way I just suggested to you....

Can you think of anyone who could help me in my project? It may become too much for me to do everything....

Now let me explain how I operate this kindergarten. My uncle kept some of my educational expenses in case of emergency. As of now, it amounts to 100 yen, and I would like to invest it. However, from my past experience, I can tell that this money will not last long. I asked people to help me support this kindergarten, but due to my lack of virtue, there are few donations from Fukaura, and from the temples I haven't even received a penny. The priests have enough money for a party with food and sakē; this amount would be sufficient to support the Mentorgarten for one week. Many boys and girls could polish their wisdom and virtue. But we are in a decadent period. Please understand the situation. I have no acquaintance except yourself to whom I can describe what I feel. Since I became a Buddhist monk, I want to dedicate my life to educate others as well as to continue my own practice at this place. If you tell me, "Come!" I will go right away. And when we meet face to face, perhaps you can guide me in two ways: First, about my own practice. Secondly, how to operate this kindergarten....

For some reason, Sōyen Shaku wrote very little back to Nyogen Senzaki. I assume that after writing the above letter, Nyogen Senzaki went to see his teacher and asked for some advice, encouragement, and support, because Sōyen Shaku wrote the following, in the fall of 1901:

Even if the blows of Tokusan's staff were to fall like rain, or if Rinzai's shout were to become louder than thunder, I would not be disturbed. Even if Furona's speech were as eloquent as a running river and Sāriputra's wisdom were as glittering as the morning star, I would not be impressed. If there were a man whose behavior was so pure that even the Puritans would admire him, if he did not have the vow to save all sentient beings, I would not respect him. However, what if I met a bodhisattva such as Jōfukyō in the Lotus Sūtra with no ego whatsoever? When he raises his hand, it becomes the hand of compassion; when he stretches his feet, they become a Moses basket of generosity. If he sees young boys and girls, it is as if they are his own children; if he sees handicapped people, it is as though they are himself; although he has no wife and children, he makes a family wherever he goes, and teaches the true Dharma to all who come to him. If he were to devote himself to the realization of Buddha-nature only, I would shed tears and not hesitate to respect him. In this day and age, among ten thousand Buddhist priests, how many are like this? Here is a monk named Nyogen. He is poor. He has no position, no fame, but he has a vow stronger than fame. His Dharma treasure is worth more than any material wealth. He has compassion, which is higher than any position. After leaving Engaku-Ji, he went into the secular world, and now he wants to establish the Mentorgarten and devote his body and mind to the young people's spiritual growth…. I, Sōyen, give one hundred percent moral support to his project. May this good student, with great vows for all, manifest both flower and fruit simultaneously.

Despite Nyogen Senzaki's hard work and his teacher's encouragement, the management of the school was not a success. In those days, he practiced *takuhatsu* (begging for alms), and whenever he was discouraged, he wrote letters to Sōyen Shaku (letters now in the archives at Tokei-Ji in Kamakura). Around 1904, when the situation became desperate, the idea of going to America to raise funds came to his mind. It happened that Sōyen Shaku had been invited by Mrs. Alexander Russell (the first woman Zen student in America) to San Francisco, to teach her small Zen group. Nyogen Senzaki was asked by his teacher to accompany him to the United States, although the purpose of their trip was quite different.

Maybe because his karma always forced him to be alone, or perhaps because by coincidence, right before leaving, Nyogen Senzaki suffered from trachoma (a highly contagious inflammation around the eye), and he had to postpone his departure. Three months later, he took a cargo ship to Seattle. From there, he traveled to San Francisco by train, where his teacher and D.T. Suzuki already were staying with the Russells. However, his time with them did not last long. For some unknown reason, after a short period, Nyogen Senzaki left the Russell house. In my opinion, this is when Nyogen Zen—the starkly simple, deeply idealistic, pure Zen that was Senzaki's gift to America—took root. At least twice during the ensuing year, according to Sōyen Shaku's diary, Nyogen Senzaki visited his master in San Francisco. I assume it was during these visits that the teacher told his student to remain in this "strange land" and adopt its new language and culture. He also told him to remain anonymous and not to teach Zen for at least seventeen years.

In 1917, Nyogen Senzaki wrote the following letter to his friend, Kishu, a Zen Buddhist monk who was also a student of Sōyen Shaku, describing his life in America:

Although I was Sōyen Shaku's worst student, my bodhicitta never weakened. Even if I don't write a letter to him for the rest of my life, this, at least, Rōshi knows. Perhaps you can ask Chussan to take this letter to Rōshi and tell him that Senzaki is still alive.

Nowadays I work from 7 P.M. throughout the night as a telephone operator and bookkeeper for this hotel. Then from 7 A.M. to 11 A.M. I work as a housekeeper, with three American women and one Italian man as assistants. The only time I can sleep is from 2 P.M. to 6 P.M., and when it is too busy, sometimes I don't sleep for two or three days. Between 2 A.M. and 5 A.M., the telephone rings less often, and during that time, I study.

Ever since I came to America, I have worked like a machine. Nevertheless, I am still having financial problems. Every day, using the typewriter, I write thirty or forty letters. The telephone operation is not only busy, but requires my full attention. On top of all this, about two hundred people are living in this hotel. Sometimes the couples fight, and I have to talk to them. Sometimes I assist the house detective in catching a thief. Other times, I have to dress up and go to the theater with some of the guests. Last night, someone came in drunk, so I hit him and took him to bed. And on and on. I work so hard; why can't I save any money? My debts increase every month, so I cannot conduct my own independent business.

Sōyen Shaku passed away on November 1st, 1919, and some time later, Nyogen Senzaki started a small Zen group in San Francisco. Around 1932, he moved from San Francisco to Los Angeles, where he met Shūbin Tanahashi, who became his first Zen student. It was she who showed him the women's magazine *Fujin Kōron* containing haiku poems and other works of Sōen Roshi. Thus the correspondence between Sōen Nakagawa and Nyogen Senzaki began, in December 1934. When war broke out in 1941, Nyogen Senzaki was sent to an internment camp at Heart Mountain, Wyoming. The correspondence between him and Sōen Roshi was interrupted until the war ended on August 15th, 1945.

Nyogen Senzaki returned to Los Angeles. One of his followers, the owner of the Miyako Hotel, offered him a room and some space to be used by his Zen group. The hotel was located near Little Tōkyō, in downtown Los Angeles. Nyogen Senzaki's correspondence with Sōen Nakagawa Roshi resumed. On Sōen Roshi's first trip to the United States in 1949, Nyogen Senzaki was still living in the Miyako Hotel. A few years later, at the suggestion of Shūbin Tanahashi, Senzaki moved his zendo and residence to a house across the street from her apartment, on Second Street. This was to be his last home.

At the age of 82, after struggling and teaching in the United States for more than fifty years, Nyogen Senzaki quietly passed away. It was May 7th, 1958. In his will, he bequeathed all his belongings to Sōen Nakagawa Rōshi. He also asked his followers to scatter his ashes in a field in California. However, this did not happen. Instead, half his ashes were buried in Evergreen Cemetery, Los Angeles. The other half were buried in Dai Bosatsu Zendo's Saṅgha Meadow cemetery, in the Catskill Mountains near Livingston Manor, New York, where they were later mixed with Sōen Rōshi's ashes. On his next trip to the United States, Sōen Rōshi moved Senzaki's belongings to Shūbin-san's house. He brought most of Senzaki's manuscripts back to Japan.

When I left Yokohama Harbor for the United States in August 1960, Sōen Rōshi came to see me off and entrusted me with three large boxes containing most of Nyogen Senzaki's manuscripts, and asked me to publish them when the possibility arose. I promised him that I would. A first selection appeared in *Namu Dai Bosa*, which was published in 1976 to celebrate the opening of Dai Bosatsu Zendo Kongō-Ji. Then, in 1978, the first edition of *Like a Dream, Like a Fantasy* was brought out. All the poems were left unedited; they were presented as they were originally written.

Nyogen Senzaki had a deep knowledge of Chinese literature and was well trained in poetry. All the poems that appear in this book were originally composed in Chinese, following the strict rules of Chinese poetry. Then Nyogen Senzaki himself translated them into English. The Chinese and English versions are, of course, quite different.

The poems in "On Sōyen Shaku" were mainly composed to commemorate his teacher's passing. Regardless of his circumstances—even when he was at the internment camp—when November came, Nyogen Senzaki conducted a memorial service and composed a poem for the occasion. In my opinion, this section speaks more than any other about the life of Nyogen Senzaki in America: loneliness, poverty, a simple life-style deeply rooted in American soil, and gratitude to his teacher.

In the second edition, upon which this Wisdom edition is based, many poems and essays from *Namu Dai Bosa* have been included. Although these writings are not in the chronological order in which they were written, I have arranged them according to significant events in the Buddhist tradition. Also, for this edition I did not include Sōyen Shaku's poems and letters addressed to his own teacher, Kōsen Imakita Rōshi. And, to avoid potential misunderstandings, some sections that could be seen as dismissive of other traditions have been edited or omitted.

For some uncanny reason, there has been a renewed interest in Nyogen Senzaki's Dharma life in the West. Visitors come from everywhere to visit his graves in Los Angeles and Dai Bosatsu Zendo. Journalists come to borrow letters and photos of him. This new edition of his writings and teachings is a concrete example. As he was inconspicuous and always wanted to remain anonymous, it is ironic that the recent Dharma movement brings Nyogen Senzaki to the forefront of Buddhism in America.

During the past two decades or so, many Western Dharma students enthusiastically requested a new edition of this book. But the time was not ready. Now I feel the readiness of time has come at last. I could no longer postpone this project. My promise that I made to Sōen Rōshi at Yokohama Harbor forty-four years ago has finally come to fruition. Through the publication of this book I trust I may be able to express my respect to Nyogen Senzaki, whom I met only once in this incarnation. Also my gratitude extends to my teacher, Sōen Nakagawa Rōshi, with whom I was associated for thirty-three years in this lifetime and who is still influencing me to this day.

Portions of this book were taken from *Namu Dai Bosa,* edited by Lou Nordstrom. The preface, slightly altered, was taken from *Endless Vow: The Zen Path of Sōen Nakagawa,* compiled and translated by Kazuaki Tanahashi and Rokō Sherry Chayat. I am thankful to these three individuals for all their efforts and their generosity. My special gratitude goes to Rokō ni Oshō for her thorough editing of the manuscript. Her efforts have been instrumental in the publication of this edition.

I would like to acknowledge the generous support of Nippon Koten Kenkyūkai in making this publication possible.

I am also grateful to my students Seigan, Fūjin, Yayoi, Genshin, Banko, Saiun, Tara, and Tina. Without their unconditional dedication, this second edition would have remained indeed "like a dream, like a fantasy."

Eidō Tai Shimano
Dai Bosatsu Zendo, Kongō-Ji, New York
Spring 2005

一人つゝ来ては月さす窓ちかく
今宵うす茶を公案にして

CHINESE POEMS

Nyogen Senzaki in front of Tōzen-Zenkutsu
Los Angeles, California

On Buddha's Birthday

From ancient times to the modern days,
Man depends on the topsy-turvy way of God or the gods,
Instead of relying on himself.
Such a flower of delusion is destined to be blown off
Even by the slightest breeze of intellectuality.
The baby Buddha, pointing one hand heavenward
And the other toward the earth,
Declared the words of independence.
"Above the heavens, beneath the earth,
I alone am the World-Honored One."
That voice has shaken whole worlds
And awakened all sentient beings.

                                          April 4, 1937

Through the five senses of man,
Buddha comes and goes, independently.
He walks freely, up and down,
North, south, east, and west.
Enchantment of spring brought us foolish ones together.
Such a childish play of the Flower Festival!

Scattering the petals like rain over the head of a doll!
What a delusion!

April 10, 1938

We have here the very same breeze as the remote spring at
    Lumbinī, the birthplace of the Buddha.
The very same mist hangs over the evening garden as it did over
    the ancient woods of Aśoka trees.
There is no spot on this good earth which is not the birthplace of
    a Buddha.
This year, without a flower house for the baby Buddha,
We celebrate the festival with two American Zen monks who
    were newly ordained.

April 14, 1940

Buddha, at his birth, walked seven steps firmly,
Looked to each of the four quarters of earth,
Declaring both freedom and independence for man.
He said, "Above the heavens, beneath the earth,
I alone am the World-Honored One."
Ever since then, the wise recognize each man as master
    of the universe,
While the unenlightened judge persons by the color of
    their faces.
Enlightenment has no concern with color, race, or wealth.
How long will mankind ignore the words of the baby Buddha,
And fight shamelessly over the yellow metal and selfish power?
Hey!

April 13, 1941

Sons and daughters of the Sun are interned
In a desert plateau, an outskirt of Heart Mountain,
Which they rendered the Mountain of Compassion
     or Loving-kindness.
They made paper flowers to celebrate Vesak, the birthday
     of Buddha.
"Above the heavens, beneath the earth, I alone am the World-
     Honored One," said the baby Buddha,
Declaring the spirit of independence and self-respect of each
     sentient being of the world.
Hey! You! Stupid sagebrush and timid cactus!
Why don't you stretch out your green buds to answer the call of
     spring?

                                        April 13, 1943

An evacuee artist carved the statue of baby Buddha.
Each of us pours the perfumed warm water
Over the head of the newly born Buddha.
The cold spell may come to an end after this.
A few grasses try to raise their heads in the tardy spring,
While the mountain peaks put on and off
Their veils of white cloud.

                                        April 9, 1944

Land of Liberty!
People of Independence!
The Constitution is beautiful.
It blooms like the spring flower.
It is the scripture by itself.

No foreign book can surpass it.
Like the baby Buddha,
Each of the people
Should point to heaven and earth, and say,
"America is the country of righteousness."

April 8, 1945

After his birth the infant Buddha walked
Four directions with seven paces.
Bravely and gracefully eight thousand times in the past,
He has come into this world and has gone from it again.
What the legend says is not strange to us at all.
Again this morning the Buddha is born
In the Western Hemisphere!
See! The flower drift of pink and white....
The springtide of the great city.
Praise be to the one, perfect in wisdom.

April 7, 1946

Again this spring
We gather flowers and decorate
The flower house for the baby Buddha.
The church bells of our community
Peal their tidings to our roof top.
Thousands of worshippers
Kneel to the ground to pay homage—
Each postulating his own legendary hero.
They should stand up as our baby Buddha
And declare their independence of thought,

Saying, "Above the heavens, beneath the earth,
I alone am the World-Honored One."

April 11, 1948

We celebrate Buddha's birth this Easter Sunday.
The face of baby Buddha is quite familiar to us
Time and space shrink into this moment.
Pointing to heaven and earth,
Buddha stands right here.
Namo Tasso Bhagavato Arahato Samma Sambuddhassa!

April 9, 1950

On Realization Day

"It is a strange but wonderful fact that all sentient beings—
Each of them has Buddha-nature, pure and perfect!"
So Buddha exclaimed when he attained realization at dawn
    in the Gaya forest.
Henceforth, he preached forty-five years to tell the truth
    to his followers.
His speeches were eloquent in Dharma,
Eloquent in reasoning,
Eloquent in words,
Eloquent in compassion,
And his voices were excellent, soft, harmonious, intellectual,
    masculine, correct,
Deep and inexhaustible.
These were, however, nothing but the repetition of his first voice
    and of his first speech
Under the Pippala tree.
Who says the anecdote was two thousand four hundred
    and sixty-nine years ago?
Listen to the actual voice within you
At this minute of the commemoration!

                        December 10, 1939

What is all this trouble with the world?
What is the matter with mankind?
Asura, the fighting devils jump and dance
On the other hemisphere.
Here is a sword of Buddha's wisdom
Which conquers all monsters of delusion,
And gives to all peace and enlightenment.

December 8, 1940

Buddha was a homeless monk of Old India.
You are the future buddhas in the New World.
In your golden silence,
There is neither time nor space.
You always live with the Enlightened One.
Namo Tasso Bhagavato Arahato Samma Sambuddhassa!

December 14, 1941

A swarm of demons infests the whole of humanity.
It resembles the scenery of Gaya where Buddha fought his last
    battle to attain realization.
We, Zen students in this internment, meditate today
To commemorate the Enlightened One.
We sit firmly in this zendo while the cold wind of the plateau
Pierces to our bones.
All demons within us freeze to death.
No more demons exist in the snowstorm
Under the Mountain of Compassion.

December 6, 1942

The frozen clouds of winter
Hung stubbornly around the Himalayan Mountain.
The dawn, however, came to Gaya,
And the effulgent light illuminated the surroundings.
It is not strange that a mediocrity became the Buddha.
Lucifer and Vesper are merely two names for Venus.[1]

December 12, 1943

Mountains and rivers do not conflict.
Grasses and trees live harmoniously.
Nature itself manifests loving-kindness.
Eighty-four thousand delusions
Cover the eyes of man.
He dreams the whole world
In a fighting mood.
He sees not the morning star
In the same way as Buddha did.
Unless he enters into deep zazen
And emancipates himself
From his own conflicts,
He cannot comprehend
The beautiful cooperation of this universe.

December 10, 1944

This world is the palace of enlightenment,
In his own place each person is a hero
Striving for what he would attain.
You also may have ideals,
Even forty-eight of them,

Only to be dispersed like early stars.
See! The new moon rules the heaven!
If you do not realize truth this moment,
It is nobody's fault but your own.

December 4, 1945

The world is beautiful
With its mountains and waters.
Man only suffers according to his ignorance.
If he realizes truth,
Glancing at the morning star
As Buddha did,
He will be peaceful and happy
Wherever he is on this good earth.

December 8, 1946

No Buddhist forgets the winter seclusion.
Buddha Śākyamuni attained realization
On the morning of the eighth of December.
Americans join the Japanese to commemorate the day.
Many other bodhisattvas are meditating with us,
Somehow, somewhere in this great city.
Hear the sound of clapper and bell
Through the dreamy mist of this strange Buddha land!

December 12, 1948

On Nirvāṇa Day

Under the Sala trees, Buddha stretched out his feet on
    his deathbed,
And said to his disciples,
"Those who say that Tathāgata enters into nirvāṇa are not
    my disciples.
Yet those who say that Tathāgata does not enter into nirvāṇa are
    also not my disciples."
Like the last words of a father to his beloved children,
Buddha emphasized these words of Zen.
It is not only a narrative of two thousand four hundred and
    twenty-two years ago,
But also our own concern this very day.
Look! The bushes outside of this humble house stretch
    their young leaves,
And the golden flowers are blooming here and there.
The spring breezes nurse gently the whole body of Tathāgata,
Which does not come from anywhere,
And which does not depart to any place.

1937

Two thousand four hundred and twenty-three years have passed
Since Buddha entered into Parinirvāṇa.
Here we see, after the spring rain, his remains in the sunny South
    of California.
Who says that his followers are degenerated?
Each drop of the fragrant dew in the garden
Shines the same as in his living days.

February 20, 1938

After his last discourse, the Buddha said,
"Now, my disciples, be quiet.
Do not speak a word.
It is time to part from you."
Buddha tried to open the minds of all disciples in silence.
His Zen was shining like the moon above the Sala forest,
    but alas!
Mahākāśyapa, his successor, being absent,
None of the remaining monks could reflect the light.
Their hearts were like broken mirrors.
The night of sadness thus passed in vain.

February 12, 1939

The branches and leaves of Buddhism grow in the southern
    countries—Ceylon, Burma, and Siam—
And the flowers of it blossom in the northern countries—
Nepal, Tibet, China, and Japan.
The original form of Theravāda
And later development of Mahāyāna
Both turn the Dharma wheel even in our days—

Two thousand four hundred and twenty-five years after
    Buddha's death.
Who knows best how to preserve the teaching of Tathāgata?
The followers of Buddha in the Orient and in the Occident
Read and study the scriptures,
And memorize and recite the precepts.
Should the teaching be maintained in this way?
I say, "Yes," and I say, "No."

February 18, 1940

Above the silent forest of Sala trees,
The full moon of February hung.
Under the pale light of that moon,
Our old teacher, the Buddha, passed away.
Impermanence always permeates our introspection,
Especially this February.
Americans are now learning perseverance, as Buddha taught,
Studying life seriously.

February 1942

"Those who live without unreasonable desires
Are walking on the road of nirvāṇa."
So Buddha said on his deathbed.
Evacuees who follow him, learning contentment,
Should attain peace of mind
Even in the frozen desert of internment.
See a break in the clouds in the East!
The winter sun rises calmly,
Illuminating the light of wisdom.

February 14, 1943

"In the spring garden of discipline,
Perseverance blooms its first flower."
So the Buddha said in his last teaching.
Hundred thousand brothers and sisters!
You have pined long enough.
Emancipation is not far from you.

                                        February 13, 1944

On his deathbed
Buddha taught his disciples
To practice forbearance.
Man should act like the willow branches,
Which bend gently against the wind.
Three times we have commemorated
Buddha's Nirvāṇa Day in this plateau.
We did not learn much during the past three years.
We are ready, however,
To face the world with equanimity,
Taking smilingly the snowstorm of abuse
As well as the sunshine of honeyed words.
Praise be to the Buddha, the Enlightened One.

                                        February 18, 1945

When Buddha passed from the world,
Ānanda and most of the good monks
Wept in grief,
While Subhadra and a few bad ones
Felt relief from discipline.
The cremation was over before sundown.

The people of ten countries built ten towers
Enshrining Buddha's remaining ashes.
The vines which cover a window of our zendo
Show us nirvāṇa today with their new buds.

February 17, 1946

In the Sala grove the disciples are sunk in grief.
Buddha gave them his last talk on how to distinguish Dharma
    from false teachings.
Are there really false teachings?
Are they not Dharma itself?
The moon shows the shadow of a tree on the ground.
Without the dark part there is no light space.
Without light space there is no shadow of a tree.
Namo Tasso Bhagavato Arahato Samma Sambuddhassa!

February 16, 1947

We commemorate Nirvāṇa Day in this foggy city,
Speaking of the birth and death of the Buddha.
Brother Sōen wrote us a letter from Japan;
He said that he is in the western zendo.
We call ours an eastern zendo.
What queer persons we monks are!
Nirvāṇa is not a place where one comes or goes.
Nirvāṇa has no trace of time which one names old or new.
What is it then?
Hey!

February 15, 1948

From ancient times to this modern age
There is only one road to nirvāṇa.
No one can possess nirvāṇa
Because it is the inner-self of each.
Nirvāṇa is not a limited place,
Anyone can reach it at any time.
Who says the city is dusty and smoggy?
The spring breeze is bringing you
The fragrance of early flowers
In this commemoration of Buddha's Nirvāṇa Day.

February 18, 1951

On Bodhidharma Day

Bodhidharma predicted the future growth of his teaching,
Telling of a flower with five petals.
That flower blooms among mankind,
Age after age, endlessly.
Here in America, and there in Europe,
The bud of the flower is recognized by the men of intuitive mind.
A Chinese ambassador, on his way home from India,
Met Bodhidharma, who was going back to the West,
So the legend says, wearing one shoe on his foot and the other
    foot bared—
He passed, trotting along.
It was one thousand four hundred and nine years ago.
No one ever saw him since, except Zen students.
Bodhidharma comes in the autumn to meet Zen students.
His old robe is a colorful brocade, woven with red and yellow
    leaves of fall.
This evening, he stays with us for a little while,
And then walks away slowly in the twilight.

October 1937

Some old papers were recently excavated
From the ruins of an ancient city
In Eastern Turkestan.
The scholars say that they contain
The thought of Bodhidharma,
And they have been busy turning out commentaries,
Both in the horizontal writing of the West,
And the vertical lines of the Orient.
Who knows exactly the thought of the blue-eyed monk?
Some imitate his zazen and gaze at the wall
Until the sun goes down.
Hey—you are all wrong!

October 9, 1938

Bodhidharma was the chief monk in this sesshin.
The nights in our zendo were pure and calm as ever.
We do not stop anyone who goes out from us.
We are, however, quite severe to those who newly come to us.
In olden times, one of Bodhidharma's disciples had to cut off his
    arm to show the teacher his sincerity.
That has been the way of patriarchs,
And that will be our path in the future.
Brother Sofu is going to Nippon, across the Pacific Ocean,
To study Shingon meditation.
He can perform his mudrā without fingers.
He can recite his dhāraṇī without voice.
Wherever he goes, he is the same old disciple of Bodhidharma,
    the blue-eyed monk of Zen.

October 13, 1940

No ships cross the Pacific Ocean from Japan.
We commemorate Bodhidharma in the loneliness of autumn.
My brother monk does not come to America,
And I do not go to Japan.
Listen to the incantation of the dhāraṇī, *The Great Compassion!*
My voice is my brother's voice!
Yes, all these voices come just from one throat.

October 12, 1941

Autumn came naturally to the exiled life.
We commemorate again Bodhidharma, our patriarch.
The four ways of conduct,* as he taught us to practice them,
Were carried by us during the past twelve months.
The seeds of Zen were planted deep
And covered well with earth.
Who knows and who cares what will happen tomorrow
     on this tricky plateau?
Before long, cold clouds may cover us, and snowstorms may visit us
With no effect on our equanimity.

October 3, 1943

*Four Ways of Conduct:
1. To know how to requite hatred with loving-kindness.
2. To acknowledge one's karma, realizing that one's present circumstances
    are the result of one's past thoughts, words, and deeds.
3. Not to crave anything.
4. To be in accord with Dharma.

In this commemoration we burn incense from Japan.
The fragrance remains with us.
Bodhidharma neither comes nor goes.
Blue eyes and black
Meditate in our zendo.

October 6, 1946

Evening clouds have vanished
Leaving the dark forest of cypress.
There is no road to the temple of Bodhidharma!
A brook runs through the fallen leaves,
The wild underbrush of autumn hides it here and there.
What was the teaching of the blue-eyed monk?
Look! The steep, rocky cliffs
Have gazed at each other
For one thousand four hundred years
Keeping the untransmissible Dharma by themselves.

October 5, 1947

Zen students practice perseverance age after age.
They climb the mountains of meditation.
They sail the seas of wisdom and knowledge.
Where is their goal?
Bodhidharma says, "I know not."
An American youth enters the monkhood.
A Japanese monk crosses the Pacific.
Who knows their purpose?
What are they going to do?
Bodhidharma says, "I know not."

October 10, 1948

Before Bodhidharma came
To China from India,
The rugged mountains of Wei
Were established in the meditation pose.
The legend says:
"Bodhidharma returned to India
Carrying one shoe in his hand."
Coming and going have nothing to do with his Zen.
Is not this chrysanthemum
A lingering scent of our master's robe?

October 9, 1949

My friends, do you say
You could not sleep last night?
The heat of this late summer bothered you;
You could not find any cooler place.
Why did Bodhidharma come to China?
The question, I know, also bothered you.
Wait until the evening sun colors the mountains
With its gentle rays....
You get more than coolness at that moment.
You meet the blue-eyed monk face to face.

October 7, 1951

Without feet Bodhidharma came from China to India;
The flower of the five petals is shapeless;
Autumn finds the coolness of Zen crossing the Atlantic.
Behold! This lotus mudrā contains the whole affair.

October 4, 1953

BODHIDHARMA

The thready limbs of the weeping willow play with the spring
   breeze. They almost touch my sleeve when I promenade
   in the soft air with Bodhidharma.
The sunset-glow of a summer day tinges my window while I
   watch the colorful clouds in the western sky, and listen to the
   whisper of Bodhidharma—a message from eternity.
The agitated wind of autumn scatters the fallen leaves in the
   garden, and the noise wakes me up at midnight. The light still
   remains burning, and I thought I spoke to Bodhidharma—
   nay, it was my own shadow.
On a winter day children play with the remaining snow. They
   make the blue-eyed snowman, Bodhidharma, but it will not
   last long. It will melt soon, reducing itself to nothingness.

Undated

On Sōyen Shaku

How can I forget his angry face?
How can I forget the blows of his strong fist?
Thirty years in America,
I worked my way to answer him—
Cultivating a Buddhist field in this strange land.
This autumn, the same as in the past,
I have no crop but the growth of my white hair.
The wind whistles like his scolding voice,
And the rain hits me,
Each drop like his whip.
Hey!

November 3, 1935

Every autumn I see his penetrating eyes in the moonlight.
Every spring I hear his kind words among the beautiful flowers.
Toward winter, as the days near his commemoration,
I light the longing lamp for him while the night rain patters
    my window.
How unreasonable my tears are!
At last, the day has come—the first day of November.

All my friends in Dharma are gathered here.
Now I can burn incense for him to pay homage to his
      whole body.

November 1, 1936

My teacher scolded me like a thunderstorm,
And he struck me with his fist.
It was merely a dream of yesterday.
He smiled at me, and expressed his kindness with a gesture.
It was also an image of fleeting illusions.
Nineteen years ago, he passed from the world, and his body was
      cremated.
What is the use of poking the remaining ashes?
Look! The moon depicts a picture of the autumn tree.
A naked branch stretches itself and casts a slanting shadow at the
      window.
Let us pay homage to the real being of Sōyen Shaku,
The pioneer Zen master in America.

November 13, 1938

Again November is here to awaken this indolent monk.
On the day of his teacher's commemoration,
Even though he is lazy and dull as an ox,
His back is covered with cold perspiration,
Nothing yet accomplished in this strange land,
He now shrinks into himself with the chilliness of the
      autumn wind,
Making nine bows, up and down,
Hitting the floor with his hoary head—
Hey! What are you doing?

There is no one who receives homage.
There is no one who pays homage.

November 12, 1939

For the first time, I received a photograph of my teacher's
    tombstone.
A brother monk of mine visited Kamakura,
Took the picture, and sent it to me.
He swept the fallen leaves from the grave
And paid homage to Sōyen Shaku.
How I envy his opportunity!
Today, here in America, we commemorate the teacher,
Twenty-one years after his death.
Hundreds of chrysanthemum flowers are offered on the altar.
The fragrance of autumn fills the cleavage between Japan
    and America.
I bow nine times to our rōshi, Sōyen Shaku.

November 10, 1940

The cold night of late autumn often disturbs my dream.
Surviving my teacher, twenty-two years,
I am still a stupid monk.
I can only follow in his footsteps,
The rest of my life.
The white chrysanthemum in the yard of this humble house
Recalls memories of the past.
Its faint fragrance comes and goes over the Pacific Ocean.

November 9, 1941

In this part of the plateau we have no woods,
No trees around us.
If the snowstorm comes to the village of honeycomb,
One may fail to tell either east or west, south or north.
Our imagination, thus, goes back to the Gobi Desert of ancient
    times,
Where many Chinese monks perished on their way to India.
Thanks to America!
The lamp of Dharma burns in the exiled life.
Today we commemorate Sōyen Shaku, the pioneer Zen teacher
    in the land of liberty.
We offer incense to his portrait, with no wild flowers,
But the fragrance of the faith.

                                        November 7, 1943

Like that moment of my presentiment of the death
    of my teacher
Suddenly I woke up last night,
Exactly twenty-five years after the event.
From the window of this cell,
I saw the stars strewn in the heavens,
Each twinkling its eternal loneliness.
I lit the lamp till dawn and mused alone.
What have I done in this strange land?
Nothing could I do without my teacher.
I have lived almost in vain,
While the teaching itself joined
To the revival of American spirit.
Praise be to the power of the wisdom of enlightenment!

                                        November 5, 1944

For forty years I have not seen
My teacher, Sōyen Shaku, in person.
I have carried his Zen in my empty fist,
Wandering ever since in this strange land.
Being a mere returnee from the evacuation
I could establish no zendo
Where his followers should commemorate
The twenty-sixth anniversary of his death.
The cold rain purifies everything on the earth
In the great city of Los Angeles, today.
I open my fist and spread the fingers
At the street corner in the evening rush hour.

October 29, 1945

The work goes on and on,
Hammering and forging
The steel of Zen.
Wherever a monk lives
The old process continues
Time after time.
Here comes another autumn dawn!
The lamp still burns
While morning rain patters at the window.
Let us pay homage to our rōshi, Sōyen Shaku.
Namo Tasso Bhagavato Arahato Samma Sambuddhassa!

November 5, 1946

As a wanderer in this strange land forty-two years,
I commemorate my teacher each autumn.
Now, on the sixth floor of this hotel,
He gazes at me as severely as ever.
"How is the work, Awkward One?"
He might be saying to me.
"America has Zen all the time.
Why, my teacher, should I meddle?"
Namo Tasso Bhagavato Arahato Samma Sambuddhassa!

November 2, 1947

My teacher used to say,
"Sweet words and material favors
Easily pull a monk down to laziness."
What have I done in my old age?
The Saṅgha takes care of me too well,
And I am tardy and slow in my work.
I am shamed to face the beautiful sunset,
The autumn wind sharply penetrates my bones.

November 7, 1948

Scolding words and iron fist are yesterday's dream.
Smiling face and kind speech are icicles in the sun.
What mountain guards my teacher's holy bones?
The moonlight slants a bare branch across the window.

November 1, 1953

The cold night of late autumn often disturbs my dreams.

I survive my teacher thirty-five years …

Still a stupid monk …

I can only follow his footsteps the rest of my life.

These white and yellow chrysanthemums recall

Memories of the past;

The faint fragrance comes and goes across the Pacific Ocean.

November 7, 1954

On Various Topics

Vesak

Every spot on the earth is the land of buddhas.
The countless buddhas exalt themselves among mankind,
From eternity to eternity.
They, all alike, reach samādhi through zazen,
Attain enlightenment, preach the Dharma,
And then enter into Parinirvāṇa,
In the Western Hemisphere as well as in the lands of the Far East.
The recitation of Pali formula has just stopped,
And the golden silence embraces a whole assembly of Vesak in
   America.
All buddhas of the ten quarters, all buddhas of past, present,
   and future are here—
In this moment at this Elysian forest.

May 14, 1938

Parting Words for Dr. Dwight Goddard

On the summit of the mountain,
No one remains to see the sunset.
The Tripiṭaka, the hundreds and hundreds of Buddhist scriptures,
Are left in an empty house under the pine trees.
Zen only sparkles when the desire for writing ceases.

Blessed is the man who cannot write anymore.
Now I do not doubt that the man attained Zen through
    the kōan,
"This Mind is the Buddha."

July 11, 1939

To Bashō

Any script, ancient or modern,
Is an instrument to express hocus.
It can be arranged into lines, perpendicular or horizontal.
Our Bashō, however, wrote some hocus which transcends script
    and form.
To produce poems of wordless word and formless form,
Man has to experience the loneliness of autumn,
Century after century.

November 22, 1939

The Phoenix

Lafcadio Hearn passed from the world thirty-six years ago.
His works have been translated into fifteen languages.
Life is short, but art is long.
Like the phoenix who arose from his own ashes,
The writing of Koizumi Yakumo continues its march through
    the struggles of mankind.

September 26, 1940

To Bashō

His straw sandals climbed the mountains
And crossed the rivers.
At the end of his journey,
The autumn wind was mercilessly cold.
He dreamed of the beautiful lake under the waning moon.
He did not wake up the next morning.
Bashō, the haiku poet, thus passed from the world, two
    hundred and forty-six years ago.
American haiku friends gather here to commemorate Bashō.
The loneliness of autumn saturates each heart as in the
    old times.

                                        November 11, 1940

Parting

Thus have I heard:
The army ordered
All Japanese faces to be evacuated
From the city of Los Angeles.
This homeless monk has nothing but a Japanese face.
He stayed here thirteen springs
Meditating with all faces
From all parts of the world,
And studied the teaching of Buddha with them.
Wherever he goes, he may form other groups
Inviting friends of all faces,
Beckoning them with the empty hands of Zen.

                                        May 7, 1942

To Shūbin Tanahashi[2]

The autumn wind of this year stirs up the people's minds, all over
the world.
Even the strong and wise men do not know what to do.
Upāsikā Shūbin walks bravely the road of Bodhi, and serves
others pleasantly.
She is a miniature of Avalokiteśvara, under the Mountain
of Compassion.

September 15, 1942

Heart Mountain[3]

Morning haze gives an illusion of California.
The east wind promises the coming of spring.
Within the snow-covered plateau of internment,
Evacuees can go no place else.
They can admire only the gorgeous sunrise
Beyond the barbed wire fence,
Above the hills and mountains.

January 1, 1943

New Year's Day

There is nothing more auspicious
Than the rising sun
On New Year's Day
In the exiled life.
Within a hundred miles of this naked desert,
Not a thing comes to sight.
Ten thousand Japanese are here

As American guests.
What are they enjoying in the day?
No one knows but themselves.
A spring breeze of laughter swings out from each cell.

January 1, 1944

Spring Message

Man makes enclosures by himself
When he thinks himself
Separated from other beings.
Bars as such should be taken off.
The sooner the better.
One hesitates and loses time in vain.
Nothing disturbs the unselfish man
Who harmonizes with heaven and earth.
He goes freely like a floating cloud
Or running rivulet—
Without fighting.

January 7, 1945

Closing the Meditation Hall

Fellow students:
Under Heart Mountain
We formed a Saṅgha for three years
And learned to practice
The wisdom of Avalokiteśvara.
The gate of the barbed wire fence opens.
You are now free

To contact other students,
Who join you to save all sentient beings
From ignorance and suffering.

August 15, 1945

ALONE ON NEW YEAR'S DAY

Like a snail I carry
My humble zendo with me.
It is not as small as it looks,
For the boundless sky joins it
When I open a window.
If one has no idea of limitation
He should enjoy real freedom.
A nameless monk may not have
New Year's callers to visit him,
But the morning sun hangs above the slums.
It will be honorable enough
To receive the golden light from the East.

January 1, 1946

MOVING DAY

A snail leaves the zendo
Carrying his own shell.
He goes along the old road
Passing under the Bodhi tree,
Stepping over fallen flowers.
On his way, he calls to spring

Speaking softly to the breeze,
"Three thousand worlds are my home!"

March 2, 1947

A BEAUTIFUL MEMORY

In a tower brushed by the wind of the Inland Sea,
My teacher and I share an evening.
When I awake I am alone in the Western Hemisphere.
More than seventy years have I been dreaming,
While on the Ālaya Sea floats the illusionary boat.

July 7, 1955

In the forest of saṃsāra a big snake swallows a little rabbit.
The bodhisattva pities them, for he loves them both.
Zen teachers scold their students, and strike them with
their fists;
For unless they love all sentient beings heartily,
They cannot perform their trick of changing silver and iron
into gold.

September 17, 1945

一人つゝ来ては月さす窓ちかく
今宵うす茶を公案にして

TRANSLATIONS:
SELECTED POEMS
OF JAKUSHITSU

Editor's Note: Jakushitsu Genkō Zenji was born in 1290, near Kyōto, Japan. After receiving the Dharma from Yakuō Tokuin Zenji, he went to China and polished his practice under the guidance of Master Chuhō (Zhong Feng, Ch.). Upon returning to Japan Jakushitsu founded Eigen Monastery, near Lake Biwa. There he spent the rest of his life with his disciples, inspiring them with his poetry. Jakushitsu passed away in 1368.

SITTING ALONE

Meditating deeply upon Dharma,
Reach the depth of the source.
Branching streams cannot compare to this source!
Sitting alone in a great silence
Even though the heavens turn and the earth is upset,
You will not even blink.

THE MOUNTAINS' FRIEND

The broad arms of this dusty world hold few true friends.
One feels the pangs of loneliness, and see—
How cold the autumn air becomes!
But no, behold, your search is ended here,
For countless mountains, blue afar, and green ones near,
Remain your friends eternal.

The Mountains in the Dawn

The moon is already hidden behind the western peak.
The sun is rising above the summit.
The frosty sky awaits dawn in cold silence.
One thousand mountains afar, and ten thousand rocks near—
All enter into one eye.

Western Peak

Highest mountain in the West,
Eighteen thousand miles from the East,
Reaching the sky and dwarfing the other peaks.
If one wishes to reach it, one is there already;
For a Zen student can make a mountain wherever
    his feet find him.

Mountain of Samādhi

This mountain has neither ugly rocks nor clumsy trees.
It raises itself ten thousand feet toward the cold heavens.
Even a stray cloud does not cling around the mountain.
Only the moon showers its pale light abundantly over
    the summit.

Window of Moonlight

Icy moon slowly rises through the blue haze of autumn dusk.
Pale and penetrating rays are flooding the world.
Neither is there future nor past, but one eternal present.
Where, then, can a sleepy monkey find lodging?

Senzaki's comment: Buddha used a monkey in a box with six windows to symbolize our minds. The six windows are eyes, nose, ears, tongue, body, and brain. When the monkey is sleeping, the six worlds—sight, sound, odor, touch, taste, and the object of thinking—disappear. When one enters into meditation, that monkey himself also disappears.

BOAT UNDER THE MOON

Silvery moon hangs high in the sky.
I ride a tiny boat in the vast and misty sea.
Moon and sea forgotten;
I forget that I have forgotten.
And before the window
I sit quietly in meditation until midnight.

PATH OF PATRIARCHS

You are the one who is going to walk the path of patriarchs.
Your brilliant intellectuality will harmonize with your sparkling
    Zen.
Do not say that no one understands you.
Are you not glad to meet me this morning?
Māṇi-jewel of Tathāgata-garbha reflects its light from heart
    to heart.
Each of us has the sword of prajñā with its vajra blade.
We can talk all day long about the unborn story,
Until the moon goes up to the east, above the mountains afar
And casts its pale beam upon the old creek.

A WAY OF ZEN

Many persons go to the East, and many persons return to the
    West.
When the tide reaches the highest point, one can hardly walk
    along the shore.
If you know the way of Zen, which cuts all streams instantly,
You can pass even the most dangerous strait with ease.

A Branch of Plum Tree

Last night one branch of plum tree blossomed in the snow.
All the world saw that the spring had come.
If you want to see this blossom,
You must climb the highest mountain.

Soundless Sound

I like bamboo as the symbol of constancy and simplicity.
I built my house deep within the grove.
Do not strike my bamboo with a piece of brick.
Perhaps the sound might be heard by other Zen monks
And cause trouble.

> *Senzaki's comment:* Kyōgen, a Chinese monk, was enlightened
> while sweeping the ground. His broom drove a piece of brick
> against a stalk of bamboo. He was awakened by the sound and
> attained realization.

Silently Cultivates

Before opening the mouth, already is spoken the message
   of Oneness.
Silent thunder shakes heavens and earth.
Iron-made cattle receive the whip and walk in the rainy field.
Grandfather's farm harvests this year's plentiful crop.

AN OLD GIANT

I was born from the blue sky.
I can see one thousand great worlds and three thousand stars
    around my feet.
How indulgently Sun and Moon run among them!
My eyebrows are all white, and I do not remember my age.

THE HUT OF RESTFULNESS

A monk in Old China dwelt on a rocky road by a spring.
He raised his empty fist when he met another monk.
I will not follow him, but will quit everything for good.
My gate is shut against the dust of the world,
And the entanglement of ivy—
And I sleep as I please without disturbance.

LONE MAN

He walks freely in the world,
And goes just one way.
From the eternal past to the eternal future,
He is alone,
No one accompanies him.
If you ask him how old he is,
He will look at you with a smile,
And point to the endless sky.

一人して眺め尽せし月さす窓ちかく
今宵うす茶を公案にして

DHARMA TALKS

Nyogen Senzaki at his last zendo in Los Angeles

Buddha's Words, Buddha's Mind

(1931)

The study of modern Buddhism may be divided into two parts: Buddha-Wacchana (Buddha's Words) and Buddha-Hridaya (Buddha's Mind).

Buddha Sākyamuni preached for forty-five years after having attained his realization. During the eight months of the dry season, he would go from place to place, accompanied by a number of disciples, exhorting people and teaching them through parables and sermons. The time of the rainy season he always spent in one place, either the house of one of his disciples or in the gardens and groves bestowed upon the Saṅgha by some of the rich laymen or laywomen. Male and female lay believers were called *upāsakas* and *upāsikās,* respectively, while monks were called *bhikṣus,* and the nuns, *bhikṣuṇīs.* Some of these lay believers understood Buddha's teaching thoroughly and clearly, practicing what they had acquired in their everyday life without renouncing the world like monks and nuns. Such lay believers served their families, their communities, and their countries, carrying the influence of Dharma into their worldly occupations.

Among these lay believers were philosophers, poets, statesmen, and kings. The current of their thought drew from other Indian philosophical ideas, and this assimilation became the general body of Buddhism. There were great monks and nuns whose profound knowledge and unselfish deeds gave strength and power to this body of teaching, helping it to progress in India. In the golden age of the teaching, the liberal and broad-minded Buddhists called themselves Mahāyāna Buddhists, labeling those who were more conservative Hinayāna Buddhists. *Mahāyāna* means "great vehicle," and *Hinayāna** means "small vehicle." Mahāyāna Buddhism emphasizes the possibility that everyone may become a Buddha in this life, while Theravāda Buddhism asserts that most must await some future life—perhaps, the next incarnation. The two currents of thoughts are both based on Buddha-Wacchana, Buddha's Words.

Buddha-Hridaya is Buddha's Mind, the very mind of enlightenment Sākyamuni attained under the Bodhi Tree at the age of thirty-five. When you open your inner eye you will attain the original source of the teaching, and then all the Buddha's teachings will become your own. For Buddhism is the teaching of realization. In awakening lies your only salvation. Unless you experience your own enlightenment, the teachings of the thousands of Mahāyāna books will be for you mere speculation. And though you may devote yourself to the Theravāda teachings, renouncing the world and living the rest of your life in a secluded monastery, unless you open your own inner gate by your own efforts, after your monkish body perishes you will have to start your endless travel in saṃsāra all over again. Unless you experience enlightenment, you will remain in the world of birth and death, and be unable to enter nirvāṇa, the condition of true happiness.

Ultimately there is no difference between Mahāyāna and Theravāda, man and woman, monk and nun; whoever strives hard enough will acquire the fruits of meditation. This is the teaching of Buddha-Hridaya.

Buddha-Wacchana and Buddha-Hridaya work together. For several hundred years after the death of the Buddha, the masters of Buddha-Wacchana were also masters of Buddha-Hridaya; but later on, this ceased to be the case, and the two became separated. Masters would specialize

---

*Editor's note: Most current writers about Buddhism instead now use the word *Theravāda*, which means "The Way of the Elders." *Theravāda* has been substituted in this text from here forward.

in one or the other, and so different lineages of scholars (part of Buddha-Wacchana) and ancestors (part of Buddha-Hridaya) came into being. The speculations and arguments of the scholars, because unenlightened, tended at times to mislead their followers; but the ancestors who carried the lamp of Dharma succeeded in preserving the pure teaching of Buddha Sākyamuni. There are now very few of these masters of Buddha-Hridaya left; they are the true teachers of meditation—and we call them Zen masters.

Zen meditation is the method of attaining Buddha-Hridaya, the brilliant enlightenment which is the highest and most essential of all Asian teachings. The study of it cannot be confined to hermitages in remote mountains, for it transcends all place, time, custom, sect, and even all life itself. It can and must be found and applied in the busiest city, as well as in the tranquillity of simple country life.

The Mentorgarten Sangha

(undated)

When I started the Mentorgarten movement[1] sixteen years ago, I wished to build a bridge of understanding between East and West. I coined the name "Mentorgarten" to express my feeling that the whole world is a beautiful garden, where everyone can associate peacefully and be mentors to each other. I used the German word *garten* instead of the English "garden" because of my fondness for Froebel's theory of the kindergarten.[2] We are all children of the Buddha, who is our ideal of supreme knowledge and moral perfection. I had no connection with any Japanese religious organization at that time; at the present time I have none, nor will any be established in the future. In 1927, when my brothers over in Japan sent me money to help make this meditation hall possible, they were not contributing to a church of any specific denomination, but rather to my single-handed striving to spread Buddhism among Americans, and to the spirit of true Saṅgha that had begun to form in America at that time.

Like a kindergarten, the Mentorgarten had no teacher, but we encouraged each other and tried to grow up as naturally as we could. Like a kindergarten nurse, sometimes I would presume to be gardener of the flowers; but I never forgot that I was a flower of that garden too. Mingling with young and old alike, I forgot my own age. I was happy then, and am still happy now, in this Mentorgarten. Why should I not remain so in the future?

The same spirit of Saṅgha found in my Mentorgarten movement may be found in early Buddhism—nay, not only in early Buddhism, but in both ancient and modern Buddhism as well. If there is true Buddhism, there is this Saṅgha spirit.

Buddhists of the world respect the Three Treasures: Buddha, as the goal of our self-cultivation; Dharma, as the principle governing our everyday life, by which we march step by step to Buddhahood; and Saṅgha, as the group of harmonious friends who follow the golden path of the Tathāgata. However, there is a tendency among some Buddhists not to respect Saṅgha as much as the other two Treasures. Ill-informed Buddhists in Japan, for example, worship Buddha almost as a god and Dharma as essentially the words of God. For them, priests and monks alone constitute Saṅgha. The truth is that priests and monks, though leaders of the Saṅgha, are still but a part of it, and by no means represent the whole Saṅgha. People forget that they themselves are Saṅgha, and instead blindly worship monks and priests. When they find out that monks and priests are not as worthy of such respect as they had thought, they lose their Saṅgha treasure completely.

When I first began lecturing to Americans on Buddhism, my aim was to spread knowledge of it much as one would spread the knowledge contained in physics or chemistry. Because I did not wish to deprive my Christian friends of their hours of worship, I never held meetings on Sundays. Gradually some of my friends decided to become Buddhists and be ordained. These ordained friends have formed their own American Saṅgha and are trying their best to make a true fellowship of Buddhist students. Anyone who understands the nature of early Buddhism will be glad our Saṅgha is progressing the way it is—slowly but properly.

I simply want to remind you of what we have been in the past and what we are going to strive for in the future. Buddhism is not only a philosophy and a science, it is a way of living virtuously. Therefore, you must practice the teaching in your everyday life. Endeavor to be a true gentleman or perfect lady before you call yourself a faithful Buddhist. Be harmonious among yourselves and always respect each other, for each of you is the future Buddha, with perfect wisdom and complete virtue. This is my sincere advice to young and old, men and women, no matter what their Buddhist affiliation.

Prajñā

(1931)

The subjects we Buddhists study are divided into three parts: *śīla,* "moral precepts"; *dhyāna,* "meditation"; and *prajñā,* "wisdom." Here we shall investigate the meaning of prajñā.

Because Buddhism is not a revealed religion, its wisdom is not derived from any supreme being. As Buddhists, we believe that we must attain wisdom through our own striving, just as we obtain scientific and philosophical knowledge only by independent effort. To attain prajñā, we engage in meditation and avoid conceptual speculation. In the areas of science and philosophy, we are always working on the assumption that the truth lies outside of us; therefore, these forms of knowledge leave our inner self untouched. Self-knowledge cannot be accomplished in this external manner. The teaching of Buddha provides us all with the key to open our inner shrine and make the brilliance of the highest wisdom our own—the wisdom Buddha called *Anuttara Samyak Sambodhi,* or "the highest teaching of the ultimate truth."

Buddha taught that there are three prajñās: the essence of prajñā, reflections of prajñā, and descriptions of prajñā. After he had become enlightened under the pipal tree, Buddha said: "All sentient beings in this world have perfect wisdom and complete virtue; the trouble is they are not aware of this. I must teach them the truth." This perfect wisdom is the essence of prajñā, which you and I and all sentient beings possess from the very beginning. If you are brave enough to strip off all your delusions, you can unite with the essence of prajñā at this very moment. However, only those who have entered deeply enough into samādhi in their meditation will be convinced by this statement. For the others, there are the other two prajñās.

For those who have no direct experience of prajñā through meditation, there are the reflections of prajñā achieved through philosophical introspection. The philosophical aspects of Buddhism were explicitly designed for this purpose. For those who have no training in philosophical introspection, there are the descriptions of prajñā transmitted by others. These descriptions at least give one the bare outlines of wisdom.

Let me illustrate what I have been saying with this analogy. Imagine a man wandering in a dream, who thinks he has lost his way. Wandering thus for many miles, suddenly he hears the ringing of his alarm clock. Upon hearing this familiar sound, he feels comforted, knowing he is not so far away from home after all. But he remains in the dream. The alarm continues to ring until at last the man opens his eyes, and realizes he had never lost his way at all, that all along he had in fact been lying comfortably in bed. What do you make of this?

The alarm clock of this story has been ringing in the real world from the very beginning. In reality there never was a road on which to be lost in the first place.

If you can hear the sound of prajñā the moment it is produced—just as one hears the alarm clock the moment it begins to ring—you have no need for the other two prajñās, and can enter directly into the essence of prajñā in your samādhi right now. If you cannot, you can still attend classes and read essays like this one, where you hear descriptions of prajñā, and keep in touch with reflections of prajñā through introspection.

A Lecture on Meditation: For Beginners

(undated)

Quietness is an element in meditation, but merely striving to attain quietness leads nowhere. It is like putting a paper bag over a cat's head: It will walk backward but will never be able to advance. A cranky old man who scolds children for making noise violates with his loud voice the very quietness he upholds. The same thing happens when one forces oneself to enter quietness. It is only when one forgets both the world of noise and the realm of quietness that one is able to enter into the kingdom of true silence. This, however is not what we are gathered here for, either. Watching movies or resting in the park is just as good as sitting in a zendo, if what you want is quietness. Strangers to a zendo usually are unable to see anything more than its atmosphere of quietness; the vastness lying beyond can only be detected by those who know what real Zen practice is all about.

You should never for a moment think that you are dwelling in quietness. You are students of *nonthinking*—what right have you to tarry in tranquillity! Just march on bravely, regulating your breath or working on your kōan. Zen meditation is the most simple method in the world for mind-training. Meditation is complicated and difficult only when one becomes more interested in one's own opinions and ideas than in disentangling oneself from all traces of dualistic thinking. As Zen Master Nanin once said: "Unless you empty your teacup, I cannot fill it."

In the beginning, you aim to empty your mind and try to drive all thoughts away. But *aiming* and *trying* are also thoughts! So aiming and trying keep you from your goal, of becoming emptiness itself. When you think you are in emptiness, you are not in emptiness. When you think you have discovered your Buddha-nature, you are far away from it. When no thought arises, there is no need to drive thoughts away. When nothing is born, nothing dies. When nothing is good, nothing is bad. What you never had, you will never miss. What you do not see does not disappear. What cannot increase cannot decrease. This is true emptiness. This is samādhi. When you enter into this condition, then you are walking in the Palace of Realization. Never to think—even for a moment—that you are enlightened: *This* is the ideal of Zen meditation.

A Thursday Night Lecture

(San Francisco, undated)

It gives me great pleasure to meditate with you all, on this the first night of the New Year.

A Zen student should be someone of very few words—the fewer the better. I could open my hands like this and close the meeting silently. But since our aim at meetings like this is to interpret Zen rather than actually to show it in action, I shall do my best to explain in words this peculiar subject called "Zen Buddhism."

I have here a Zen poem by Jakushitsu; the English translation goes:

> Didn't I tell you it was there?
> You could have found it without trouble, after all.
> The south wind is warm;
> The sun shines peacefully;

The birds warble their glad songs.
Spring blossoms in the treetops.

But now let's translate this poem into simpler, up-to-the-minute San Francisco language: "Happy New Year to you all!" This is what it's saying, right?

Once upon a time a student of Buddhism asked his master: "What is
the one straight passage to Buddhism?" The master replied with a Chinese word meaning "most intimate." Very simple dialogue, no? In
another anecdote, a master was asked: "What is Buddhism?" The master
answered with a word meaning "Walk on!" or "Go on!" Or in good old
American slang—"Beat it!"

Another master was asked, "Where is your Buddhism?" and he
answered, "Everywhere." So you see, Buddhism always expresses itself in
the shortest way possible—"no word at all" would be best of all. As I said
before, I could open my hands like this and bid you all good night. But
this would be to imitate another master's method of teaching, and—perhaps unfortunately for me—this is not allowed in Buddhism. You must
create your own thought and express it in your own words. What you say
must come directly from your own inner self.

The most intimate relative of yours is "you." One cannot get rid of
oneself. You may estrange your friends; forget your brothers and sisters;
drive away your children; run away from your parents; divorce your wife
or husband. But how in the world can you get rid of yourself! One must
solve one's own problems and work out one's own emancipation by oneself. The only way to open the gate of Buddhism is to use your own working mind as the precious key.

Buddhism does not believe in the existence of some "Supreme Being."
It worships nothing but the inner self of each and every one of us. A student of Buddhism should not ask anyone for help in acquiring enlightenment. If one works hard and strives constantly, one cannot but attain
emancipation. Is this not the most intimate, the most straightforward
passage for everyone?

Buddhism is the most bold and radical form of all freethinking. In Buddhism, thought, word, and action are one. It is no wonder, then, that the master said, "Walk on!" when asked "What is Buddhism?" A thought without action is a wasted corpse; a word without thought and action is a dead, useless word.[3]

Man is like a bicyclist: He is safe from falling only as long as he keeps on going. If we hold our will like an iron wall against all kinds of trouble, if our breathing is in harmony with the rhythm of right-mindedness, every action of ours will become part of the progressive current of the universe, and we will see Buddhism around us wherever we are. Then if anyone asks us where our Buddhism is, we can reply: "Our Buddhism is everywhere."

Meditating in the Realization*

(undated)

"Meditation itself is realization."
Do not aim to attain realization through meditation. You are meditating in the realization.

"Form itself is faith."
Do not aim to fulfill faith through the form of meditation. The form of meditation is nothing but faith itself.

"Activity is the path."
There is no holy power which can be called faith. Command your activity. Activity itself is the path.

---

*The words in quotation marks are statements by Jihō Sugawara, Abbot of Kenchō-Ji in Kamakura; the non-quoted words are Nyogen Senzaki's comments. They are based on a piece of calligraphy by Sugawara Rōshi. He and Nyogen Senzaki were contemporaries.

"What is Zen? It is to calm yourself and control your breathing, until you become others and others become you."

American Buddhism

(1932)

Ever since April 8 of last year we have met twice a week in this meditation hall to study Buddhism. Presuming to be the senior student, I have tried my best—despite my awkward English[4]—to introduce the teachings of Buddha to the Western mind. I appreciate very much your sincerity and eagerness as fellow students in this class, and hope you all continue your noble work as bodhisattvas, seeking ultimate truth, enlightening yourselves so as to enlighten others.

Since the good year in which most of us became acquainted with each other is going to end soon, let us look back on the progress of Buddhism in America—especially of Zen Buddhism—and consider our situation as pioneering thinkers of this historical epoch.

Modern religions must keep pace with science and human reasoning generally; otherwise, they lose their authority and perish. The true value of a religion should be judged by the brightness of its mirror of reason; it should satisfy the intellect of whoever studies it. It should also be judged by its ability to harmonize with actual life. Zen Buddhism is the very exemplar of these requirements; this is why it has proved so appealing to the young and sound-minded thinkers of America.

Zen is the essence of the teaching of Buddha. Its claim to authority is based on the fact that it derives from the mainstream of Buddha-Dharma (the transmission of Mind reaching from Buddha Sākyamuni to present-day Zen masters). Therefore, those who are interested in studying Buddhism should begin by studying Zen and its compact, direct way to true understanding.

It was but a short time ago that many Westerners thought of Buddhism as the worship of idols, natural powers, ancestral souls, and spirits. Such ideas now belong to the past. The world has progressed rapidly since then. No one these days would doubt that Buddhism is a religion based on reason, that its profound wisdom penetrates into all areas of life. Zen, because it is the actualization of this teaching, is most decidedly the Buddhism of today, and should continue to be the Buddhism of tomorrow.

During the course of time some parts of Buddhism degenerated into mere philosophical speculation, and others became tainted with monotheism or polytheism. A great majority of Buddhists—like the followers of other religions—have lost the keeness of their critical faculties, and so have retarded their own progress in the attainment of true wisdom. (Even Japanese Buddhism is year by year becoming weaker as a result of these tendencies.) Fortunately enough, however, Japanese Zen Buddhism, since the Kamakura period (beginning 1192 A.D.), always had the support of the intellectual classes, and so has been protected from pollution by alien and impure elements. Because of this continued support, Zen continues to cast the pure, brilliant light of the Lamp of Dharma even to this day.

Zen is based on self-evident fact, and so can convince anyone at any time. Because it is based on fact, Zen can pass freely through the gates of the innumerable teachings of the world; it offers no resistance and poses no threat, since its foundation is completely nondogmatic. The brighter one polishes one's mind-mirror of reason, the more this true value of Zen can be appreciated. Because Zen is fact and not "religion" in the conventional sense of the term, the American mind, with its scientific cast, takes to it very readily, whereas other religions of an emotional nature do not have a lasting influence. The alert adaptability of the American mind finds in Zen a quite congenial form of spiritual practice.

It is already possible to make comparisons between American and European Buddhism at this point in the early twentieth century. We can say that, unlike European Buddhism, American Buddhism is not scholastic in character, whereas European Buddhism is almost exclusively so.

After India became annexed to the British Empire, English scholars—both philologists and archaeologists—brought to the study of Buddhism their own particular point of view. The voice of these scholars soon echoed across the Atlantic and was heard by American thinkers. Out of this exchange came books like Henry Warren's *Buddhism in Translation* and Edwin Arnold's *Light of Asia*, as well as Paul Carus's *Gospel of Buddha* and L. Adams Beck's *Splendor of Asia*. Through these books the meaning of Buddhism as a religion of true peacefulness was brought home to the American public.

The American mind is more inclined to practical activity than to philosophical speculation. Since the Buddhism of Europe is predominantly scholastic and philosophical, it does not appeal to these people of practicality. When Theravāda Buddhism was first introduced to this country, it had only an extremely small following. It was only after Mahāyāna Buddhism had begun to be introduced that Buddhist teaching became acceptable to a larger number of people—but still the appeal was only to a very few students of the occult. Zen, because of its strong practical basis, is the Buddhism Americans can understand and practice.

Modern Americans are longing to reach the spirit of Buddha by engaging, if possible, in the actual practice the Buddha followed to attain enlightenment. Zen is the very spirit of Buddhism, the heart that beats and throbs with life, the very thing Americans long to reach. It can only be reached through practical action in one's everyday tasks.

The most beautiful part of a religion is its practical faith, not its philosophical argumentation. The American thinker requires that faith walk hand in hand with reason; only in this way can it be harmonized with the practical world. The mere postulation of dogmas and creeds will never be approved of by the majority of Americans. Therefore, unlike European scholastic Buddhism, American Buddhism must be built upon a practical foundation.

Some sixty years ago H.P. Blavatsky established her Theosophical Society for the practice of the kind of esoteric Buddhism she had learned from trans-Himalayan masters. After her death, strange elements from different cults began to creep in and corrupt the practice, until eventually the movement ceased keeping pace with modern science and philosophy, thereby disqualifying itself as a possible foundation for American Buddhism.

In keeping with their reaction against sacerdotalism, the young thinkers of America are dreaming of a religion of practicality, which is precisely what Zen is. Before any books about it were written, the seeds of Zen existed already among American students; it was only because the soil of their mind was already of sufficient richness to nourish these seeds that the books which have been written have had the effect they have had on the American public. Unlike the Shin sect of Japanese Buddhism, for example, which has various churches scattered throughout the cities and towns of California, Zen emphasizes self-reliance and self-realization, rather than a dependence on the supernatural power of God or Buddha; for this reason the teaching of Zen Buddhism has more hope of spreading in the future among Americans, for whom self-reliance is the essence of their way of life.

The America of today has many kinds of teaching. People who are interested in Zen are still but a small portion of the non-Christian groups, but the important thing is not the size of the following, but rather that Zen teaching is being sought by Americans from the very depths of their hearts. Their interest is not the result of propaganda of any sort, whether from Japan or any other foreign country. That the future of Zen in America is one of rapid growth is not difficult to foresee.

Happy New Year to you all!

The Ten Realms and the Six Pāramitās

(November 23, 1933)

Bodhisattvas: We are all buddhas—our minds and bodies are manifestations of loving-kindness itself. But through introspection, we see many stages of mental conditions which are, according to Buddhist philosophy, generally classified into ten parts. If we count them from the bottom, the lowest, they go as follows:

1. *Naraka*—hell
2. *Preta*—the suffering of greediness
3. *Tiryagyoni*—the animal mind
4. *Asura*—the fighting devils
5. *Manushya*—human beings
6. *Deva*—the gods
7. *Śrāvakas*—the actual disciples of Buddha
8. *Pratyeka Buddha*—the higher philosophers
9. *Bodhisattva*—the truth-seekers of the Mahāyāna teaching
10. *Buddha*—the Enlightened One

Reading this, you are now in the stage of *bodhisattva,* the second from the top, and the ninth above the bottom. *Bodhi* means the true path to buddhahood. A Maharaja of Benares once said, "There is no religion higher than truth." Now I say, "There is no truth higher than Buddha-Dharma." Buddhist teaching is called *Anuttara Samyak Sambodhi,* meaning, "utmost and ultimate truth which is far above all wisdoms in the world." We bodhisattvas seek this truth and nothing else.

Sattva means living being. Therefore, the lower ranks could also be called *sattvas.* But they do not seek this ultimate truth. They all think that they are in fine condition. Especially those in the lower six classes never understand how imperfect they are. They think that they are leading a proper life, and they never try to climb up to the higher stages. Buddha called these six *sattvas-samscritam,* meaning, "completely formed idea"—

a somewhat sarcastic term for those who believe themselves to be completely formed. But in the eye of Buddha, they are clinging to illusions and never will know the real truth.

Among the ten classes, the higher four are called *asamscritam*—the exact opposite word of *samscritam*. You will notice that the Sanksrit prefix *a-* takes the place of *un-* or *im-* in English. Now the disciples of Buddha, the philosophers and the bodhisattvas, know that the world is after all an illusion. It is not perfectly formed—not samscritam, but asamscritam.

These ten stages are the names of the conditions of our minds. When you first get up in the morning you are very calm and quiet; you think neither of good nor bad. Physically and mentally, you are in a normal condition. That is the stage of *manushya*. Man or woman, wise or stupid, rich or poor, this waking moment is the same. If your surroundings are agreeable to you and you are enjoying the comforts of life, you are in the sage of *deva*. You can stay in that stage longer if you know how to manage your own mind, for it is not the surroundings but your mental attitude that makes you happy or miserable.

We Buddhists do not believe in the providence of a supreme being. We are the makers of our fortune. Each person is the captain of his or her own ship. God or gods can do nothing when one steers one's own ship of karma. In the journey of life, we should watch our own steps. If we fall down, it is our own fault, and we cannot blame anyone but ourselves.

People make their own stages—suffering in *naraka* and *preta*, darkening their way in *tiryagyoni*, and fighting in the stage of *asura*. Some may stay in a condition for a few minutes, others may go up and down many times a day—passing through all the stages of mind. This is due to their evil passions—hatred, anger, greed, and the like. Until the entanglement of these attachments dissolves into nothingness, life never ceases to be suffering.

Fortunately we now understand how to proceed toward Buddhahood. In our study of Dharma, in our Buddhist morality, and in our zazen practice, we are walking the Way—day after day, step by step. This is no other than our stage of bodhisattva.

We bodhisattvas have six virtues to be accomplished. We call them the six pāramitās. *Pāramitā* in one sense means "deliverance." We deliver ourselves from the shore of samscritam to the opposite shore of asam-scritam. That is, we pass through the river of delusions and, leaving the six lower classes behind us, we reach the higher shore of the four asam-scritam. But we must not stay at the stage of *śrāvakas* and *pratyeka buddha*. We must enter the region of bodhisattvahood and seek the Buddha as our goal.

The six pāramitās are:
1. *Dana*—giving
2. *Śīla*—morality
3. *Kshānti*—perserverence
4. *Virya*—courage
5. *Dhyāna*—meditation
6. *Prajñā*—wisdom

If you give away everything you have, the whole world will be yours. In Buddhism, the most precious gift is considered to be the gift of Dharma. If you have acquired your realization, you must endeavor to spread Dharma to all beings. This is called real *dāna pāramitā*.

Śīla pāramitā is to keep the precepts of moral and ethical living. When you keep the precepts perfectly, you forget that you are keeping them, and then you are an ideal disciple of Buddha. Your śīla pāramitā will be fulfilled at that time.

Kshānti pāramitā is perseverance. With the virtue of perseverance you will accomplish the hard work needed for emancipation.

Virya pāramitā is courage. You might think that to study Buddhism one need not be brave. On the contrary, to break up your delusions you must be brave enough not to be afraid of anything. You will experience this fact when you study zazen.

Dhyāna pāramitā is zazen. This alone may lead you into the realm of realization.

Prajñā pāramitā is wisdom.

Bodhisattvas should learn and practice these six pāramitās. The motive for study should always be for the benefit of others—not for ourselves. That is, to enlighten the lower classes of Buddhist mind-stages we learn the six pāramitās. We want to save the lower sattvas from suffering and ignorance. This is the right aim according to the Mahāyāna teaching.

Zen and American Life

(undated)

Like a living current of vivid thought, Zen flows throughout our everyday life. You can touch it in ordinary conversation as well as in scholarly books. Sometimes a mere word expresses Zen almost too much; sometimes a silent mood speaks Zen quite loudly. When you sip tea smilingly, your cup may be brimful of Zen; when you have a spring breeze for your companion, you meet Zen face to face under the window. We have all had Zen from the very beginning; but unless the hinges of our minds turn gracefully to open our hearts, so that I can see myself in you and you yourself in me, there will be no Zen at all—no matter how long I speak, nor how patiently you listen.

Some of you may think of Zen as a sort of mysticism, but it is not at all a strange cult. In it there is neither miracle nor hocus-pocus. It is a way of life that all of you can experience. One who studies Zen controls one's surroundings and never is controlled by them—that's all there is to it! I carry my *nyoi* the way an Englishman carries his cane. The word *nyoi* means "obedient servant"—it never complains, no matter how hot or cold it gets; it follows me wherever I go; it always meditates with me, and never engages in noisy argument. If I speak of entering into this *nyoi*, you would probably classify me as one of those Indian fakirs, or wonder how a stout monk like me could perform such a feat. In the Zen sense, I enter the *nyoi* when there is no *nyoi* separate from me, and when I am no longer separate from it. Unification is the key with which to unlock the door of Zen.

Here is a story to help make my meaning clearer. There once was a man who had a beard fifteen inches long. He was very proud of it and was always smoothing it down and caressing it. One day a friend asked him whether he slept with his beard outside or inside the bedclothes. He was unable to answer. That night he experimented, first with his beard outside, then with it inside, but he could not remember where he kept it; nor could he decide which would be the best way! The beard he had been so proud of became a troublesome burden, and he was unable to sleep because of it.

When the mind functions smoothly, one is unaware of its functioning. An expert golfer forgets he is playing golf; a true poet forgets he has pen in hand, allowing the beautiful thoughts that flood his mind to weave their own brocade upon the page. Zen will make you an expert in the game of life. Thinking rightly, without hesitation, you will be able to live rightly, without embarrassment.

Zen is not a religion based on faith; nor is it some sort of speculative philosophy. It is the actualization of the unselfish life. The German scholar Rudolf Otto has said: "Zen monks are practical mystics. Their work is their religion and their religion is their work." In this regard, they are much like the Benedictine monks of the Middle Ages in Europe, who combined worship with labor as well.

Zen is not restricted to monasteries; it pervades everyday life and is found particularly in the area of the artistic. In Japanese culture it is everywhere—in *cha-no-yu* (the art of tea); in *ikebana* (the art of flower arrangement); in literature; in arts and crafts; and in the martial arts. It is not at all something unusual in Japan. Even boys and girls of high-school age practice Zen. This mind training will be continued throughout college and in their careers as well.

American ministers have tried in vain to convert young Japanese to modern clerical Christianity. They are wasting their time and labor! The reason for this has been well put by D.T. Suzuki in "Is Zen a Religion?"

> It is not a religion in the sense that the term is popularly understood; for Zen has no God to worship, no ceremonial rites to observe, no future abode to which the dead are destined, and, last of all, Zen has no soul whose welfare is to be looked after by somebody else. Zen is free from all these dogmatic and "religious" encumbrances.[5]

This is why Zen students make such tough customers for Christian missionaries!

Confucius said:

> At fifteen I had my mind bent on learning. At thirty I stood firm. At forty I had no doubts. At fifty I knew the decrees of heaven. At sixty my ear was an obedient organ for the reception of truth. At seventy I could follow what my heart desired without transgressing against what was right.

Buddhists don't want to wait until they are seventy before accomplishing their mind training! So as Buddha said:

> If you are brave enough to strip off your delusions, you will be Buddha at that moment; but if you cling to the lukewarm teachings to which you are attracted because of your own selfish ideas, and walk back and forth in the blind alleys of faiths and beliefs of various kinds, you will never be able to get your emancipation.

The true aim of Buddhism is realization and nothing else. In the course of time, however, Buddhism degenerated and became like other religions: an elaborate religious system was formed, and strange, impure elements came to be introduced which distorted the original teaching. Modern Japanese Buddhist sects exhibit this tendency to stray from the essence of Buddhism. But true Zen preserves the essence of Buddhism, which is none other than the fact of Buddha's enlightenment. So I dare say, if you wish to study Japanese Buddhism, study Zen first!

In general, "pious" Christians are unable to enter the gate of Zen, because they cling too much to religious conventions. Of course, there have been exceptions—Richard of St. Victor,[6] for example, who said: "If thou wishest to search out the deep things of God, search out the depths of thine own spirit." The French novelist Victor Hugo expressed the same idea by saying: "The way to ascend to God is to descend into oneself." These quotations express the first stage of Zen. In Meister Eckhardt's saying, "The eye with which I see God is the eye with which God sees me," we get a glimpse of still higher stages of Zen (which Meister Eckhardt was able to enter into without difficulty). So apparently it is not impossible for Christians to understand Zen—just very difficult.

When I first came to this country I was told that America had no philosophy of its own; that its thought was a merely derivative reflection of the thought of other countries and cultures. But I have found out that this is not really true. America has had philosophers as well as original thinkers who were true makers of history, even though their influence may not yet have extended abroad. In particular, I have in mind the American freethinkers, from Thomas Paine to Robert Ingersoll, whose books I enjoy reading very much. I also admire a great deal the American Transcendentalism of Ralph Waldo Emerson. It was after having read these writers and philosophers that I at last came upon William James's Pragmatism—the philosophy of practicality, the gospel of energy, whose chief criterion is success. Zen and American Pragmatism have much in common. Just as Pragmatism, according to James, was a new name for an old thought, so I say Zen is an old name for a new thought!

Americans in general are lovers of freedom and equality; for this reason, they make natural Zen students. There are eight aspects of American life and character that make America fertile ground for Zen:

1. American philosophy is practical.
2. American life does not cling to formality.
3. The majority of Americans are optimists.
4. Americans love nature.
5. They are capable of simple living, being both practical and efficient.
6. Americans consider true happiness to lie in universal brotherhood.
7. The American conception of ethics is rooted in individual morality.
8. Americans are rational thinkers.

Pragmatism is truly an indigenous American philosophy. At the same time, however, it is but another name for one manifestation of the sparkling rays of Zen in the actual, practical world.

Karma

(1933)

One of the great doctrines upon which Buddhist thought is based—and one of the easiest to comprehend—is the law of causation. Another name for this is the doctrine of karma. Everything takes place in accordance with this fixed and unalterable law.

The easy, casual methods of dealing with the problems of life, which seem to satisfy most people, do not satisfy the Buddhist. In Buddhism we understand that in all of life there is nothing haphazard. We understand that nothing happens except in accordance with natural laws;

that nothing can set aside the working of the eternal law of cause and effect. Miracles—if by such is implied the reversal of the fixed laws of nature—cannot occur. What seem to be miracles turn out, upon careful and unexcited examination, to be attributable to natural causes.

Every action brings its own result, in the moral as well as in the natural world. An ill-conducted business will of necessity come to grief; a badly tilled field will yield only a poor crop. According to Buddhist teaching, each of us is responsible, not only for all of our actions during the present life, but also the manner in which we embark upon each future life. Since our karma determines how and in what state we shall be born, it is inappropriate for us to blame chance or circumstance for any misfortunes that may befall us.

Another fundamental principle of Buddhism is the doctrine of the continuity of life and death. There is no sharp dividing line between this life and the next. In this sense, life is eternal. It does not begin with birth and end with death. Yet we cannot say that life persists eternally, even though it began with birth. For it makes no sense to say that life is eternal, but has a beginning.

For the Buddhist, the only significant death is the death of suffering. The body's death is considered unimportant, since it simply means rebirth. The karma continues lifetime after lifetime. An individual life is, therefore, not something in itself; it is not, as the Buddhist would put the matter, a substance, entity, or *atman*. An individual life is, in fact, nothing but karma; that is, nothing but the effect of prior deeds. Human life may be defined as a form of activity conditioned by the preservation from past lives, and the transference to future lives, of the karmic consequences of actions. By deeds is a person's character shaped; in deeds it finds its fundamental expression.

Death does not disturb the continuity of life; for karma and rebirth are continuous, the one implying and being inseparable from the other. As sin and suffering bring death, so does death bring rebirth. To attain nirvāṇa, however, is to attain a state in which there is no more birth and no more death.

Buddhism counsels independence of thought. Buddha inaugurated a religion which, instead of forcing the mind to remain within the boundaries of narrow creeds, actually encourages freethinking. Buddha's teachings revealed the underlying truth, throwing a new and startling light on the mystery of life and death. No longer a baffling riddle, life becomes a wonderful gift that each of us may shape for ourselves as we will. We may ruin our lives by wrongdoing, or we may make of them a beautiful thing. Each of us is master of ourselves and of our fate. We ourselves hold the key to the mystery of life. Though veil after veil may have to fall away before we stand face to face with the pure truth, there is no veil so dark we cannot pierce it.

As soon as we take upon ourselves responsibility for all that has been and all that is to be, we have made the first step toward the supreme end. Only within ourselves—nowhere else—lie dormant the strength and power by which we can attain perfect wisdom. We have within ourselves faculties hidden and unimagined, potentialities vaster than it is possible to measure, which when developed to their full extent, will make of us wholly enlightened beings, even as the Buddha himself.

Karma, Ālaya, and Tathatā

(undated)

Buddhism can be divided into two general parts. In Japanese, the words for these are *jissō-ron* (Buddhist ontology) and *engi-ron* (Buddhist phenomenalism). Listening to what I have to say about these two subdivisions, those more advanced in their study of Buddhism will be given the opportunity to refresh their memories, while those who are just beginning will have a chance to get a basic idea of what Buddhism is.

Jissō-ron addresses itself to the question "What is it?" Engi-ron answers the question "Why is it?" If you want to know what this universe is, what human nature is, and what you yourselves are, you study jissō-ron; if you want to know why we are here in this world, why we were born, and why we have to die, you study engi-ron.

By way of illustration I shall speak of the "I"—my own being. My body is "I" when I observe myself by means of the senses; but my mind is "I" when I experience myself through introspection. If you identify the "I" with the body exclusively, you are quite mistaken; for as you know, your body comes and goes, not only at birth and death, but every minute of every day. Is it not a fact that you lose some of your body every day, which you replace by eating? Is it not also a fact that after a seven-year cycle has been completed, you get what amounts to an entirely new body because every cell has been replaced? But if your body were your self, then you would lose and gain your self; you would regain a totally new self every seven years, which is absurd. Whatever you are, the fact of the matter is that this "you" remains unchanged, more or less by definition. Though in another body, the "I" remembers the changes that have taken place, despite the fact that the brain that remembers is entirely different from the one possessed at those earlier times. So, assuming that "you" refers to something constant, it seems clear that you are not your body.

Like the shopping crowd one sees on any Main Street in America, the elements of my body are continually passing away at every moment. No part of my body is the same as it was seven years ago; all the parts of my present body will have passed away seven years from now. Therefore I cannot claim this body as mine, nor identify myself with it. For a vegetarian like me, this body is nothing but a sackful of vegetables and grains—quite a big sackful at that! The body is merely another form of food.

What is this "I," then?

Jissō-ron's answer is that the "I" is mind. But in order to understand this answer, it is necessary to ask another question: Why is there such a thing as mind in the first place? For an answer to this question, we must turn to engi-ron.

According to Buddhist doctrine, mind is an endless chain of three processes: craving, acting, and suffering. Craving causes acting; acting causes suffering; and suffering causes more craving, and so on, on and on.... Without these three endless processes, there would be no mind. This analysis may be extended to the entire universe as well; for everything can be subsumed under these three processes, which take place in accordance with the universal law of causation. Outside of this endless chain of processes, there is nothing—certainly no such thing as a "Creator" or "Universal Ruler"!

It may be said that in Buddhism the center of the universe is a transcendental subjectivity, whereas in other religions, it is a transcendent objectivity—something existing completely outside of mind (as defined above). To a Buddhist, you yourself are the creator of the world; "you" and "the world" are but two names for the same thing, and the thing itself is Mind.

One important consequence of the view that we are the creators of the world is that we are thereby forced to recognize that we suffer by our own hands, as a result of our own actions, which are in turn the result of our cravings. We are the boss of our own fortune, the captain of our own ship. There is no original sin. There is only one's own karma, which is in no sense "original" (since it is nothing but the product of actions past and present). So we have no one to blame but ourselves; and, ultimately, no one else to be responsible for. Just as you do not suffer because of the sins of others, so you need not suffer for the sake of others' sins.

Buddhism teaches that we are living in an endless world—the world of our karmic life—a world comprised of the endless processes of craving, acting, and suffering. Unlike other religions, according to which life comes to a final end after the Last Judgment, in Buddhism there is no last-act curtain. (The Buddhist conception of time is circular, not linear.) For the Buddhist, life is an endless performance: the sort of role one plays is in the last analysis the sort of role one chooses to play.

The trouble with the concept of karma as usually explained is that its formulation requires a dualistic separation of mind and body. But if you separate mind and body, you will never be able to understand the relationship between yourself and the universe. (The relationship between your mind and your body is not different from that between you and the universe.) What is needed is a nondualistic conception of karma. This is where *ālaya* and the "ālaya process" come in. *Ālaya* means "storehouse," and it is in this storehouse that the creative power of mind is kept.

The traditional problem associated with the concept of karma has to do with the question, "What sustains the karmic process after the body has perished?" To say the carrier is called the "cosmic body" is dualistic, since even a cosmic body implies a mind as something separate. What the ālaya theory tries to achieve is a monistic explanation.

The starting point of this explanation is the rejection of materialism in favor of an immaterialist point of view. According to the ālaya theory, mind is the reflection of stored consciousness. Although the six organs produce the six senses (as in the materialistic theory), the six senses are "sorted" and "arranged" by an immaterial power known as *manas,* which in turn is nothing but a reflection of ālaya. When this creative power of mind is still in the storehouse and has not yet manifested itself, we speak of "invisible seed"; when it appears, of "visible action." Just as in dreams there is subjectivity and objectivity, so in the inner world of ālaya the invisible seed corresponds to the subjectivity of dreamland, visible action to the objectivity of dreamland. Invisible seeds produce visible actions, and in turn such actions produce new seeds in the inner world.

Ālaya is the inner self or essence; from this the mind and body are produced, as is the universe itself. I have my own world—I am my own world; you each have and are your own individual world too. All of these worlds are nothing but reflections of our own inner ālaya. I am reminded here of Einstein's statement: "Each person is the center of the universe."

The ālaya theory is a monism of self-creation; that is, according to it, the world is your creation—you can change it, rebuild and improve upon it, to suit your own will. If we think of this world as having been created by some "Supreme Being," then we become powerless to change it; we have no other alternative but to consign our fate to the mercy of the "Creator."

Ālaya is not ultimate reality; it is in turn supported by what is known as *Tathatā* (in Sanskrit) or *shinnyo* (in Japanese). Shinnyo means "reality," "noumenon" or "absoluteness." Ālaya is like the waves in the ocean, while shinnyo itself is like the water of the ocean. The waves do not derive from the water; rather, the water itself is the waves (and conversely). Each individual mind is a manifestation of shinnyo, or "Universal Mind." When we fail to realize this, we mistakenly postulate the idea of self-limited entities called "minds" separated from Universal Mind, and to this misconception of the nature of things we give the name "soul."

Buddhism educates by progressing from simplicity to complexity: in the beginning, the notion of karma, then ālaya, and finally, shinnyo. When we reach the level of shinnyo, jissō-ron and engi-ron merge; the answer to "What is it?" becomes the same as the answer to "Why is it?" When this stage is reached, phenomenon becomes noumenon, and noumenon, phenomenon. It is in this mutual identity that we find the ultimate nature of Buddha-Dharma.

The shinnyo conception provides the theoretical basis for understanding how one could become Buddha (by merging with Universal Mind). Shinnyo is the basic foundation underlying all Japanese sects and schools of modern Buddhism. (Because of the great deal of apparent contradiction among these sects and schools, however, it may take one considerable study to find this out!)

Unlike a god, shinnyo should not be an object of belief or superstition. (But in the past fifty years, Japanese living in California have constructed more than fifty Buddhist temples—it would seem that Buddhists can be as superstitious as Christians!) Simple-minded people worship God or Buddha, and are motivated merely by selfishness in their worship. But those who are able to see the light and brilliance of true wisdom and everlasting loving-kindness do not worship any external God or Buddha at all; they attain real peace and happiness at home in their everyday lives, without needing to go to a church or temple. There are many such people in this world, and they are the founders of the true universal brotherhood. I only hope the knowledge you have obtained by listening to this talk, fragmentary though it be, may provide you all with the key to those invisible shrines that exist behind and beyond the splendid visible ones of Japan and California. It would be better still if you forgot all about this talk and entered immediately into the spirit of true Buddhism in your meditation *at this very moment*. Then there would be no need for any more talk at all!

Mind and Body

(1933)

Your body is not you. Still we cling to this body as if it were. Why? We all think we own our bodies, that our bodies belong to us. But *where* is this "you" who owns this body?

"My mind is what owns this body," some of you may answer. Very well—but *where* is this "mind"! Your so-called "mind" actually reduces to four elements: sensation, perception, mental activity, and consciousness. Sensation appears when the six sense organs (including consciousness) make contact with the external world. Without this contact, there can be no such thing as sensation, nor can there be an external world. The two come into being simultaneously. When you close your eyes, there is no world of color and form; when you close your ears, no world of sound; and when you hold your nose, no world of odor. Similarly, if you have no sense of your body, there is no world of the tangible and the tactile; if you have no tongue, no world of sapidity; and if you have no brain, of course, no world of thought. Your so-called "senses" are in reality nothing but empty terms or relations. Since they are nothing in and of themselves, how can you claim them as yours? Your perception, mental activity, and consciousness are merely functions or combined powers of the six senses; and if the senses are empty, so are their functions. You cannot claim these functions as your own either; nor can you identify yourself with them. Therefore neither your body nor your mind is you.

But this shows only the negative side of Buddhism. Even though students may become emancipated from attachment to self (which is the purpose of some Buddhist practices), they are still far away from the positive side of Buddhism, which the Buddha expressed by saying, "All sentient beings have perfect wisdom and complete virtue."

Once upon a time a monk was sitting in meditation, when a woman passed in front of him. The woman was running away from her husband. When the husband came to the monk and asked him if he had seen his wife, the monk answered: "I saw only a set of bones passing by." That is a nihilistic point of view! Negative, detached, but without wisdom or compassion. With an attitude like that the monk was unable either to rescue the woman or calm the husband. So of what use is such a point of view?

Here is another story. Once there was an old lady who was very kind to a monk. She gave him a little house to live in and even looked after his food and clothing. Twenty years passed. He kept meditating from morning till night, and she continued her devoted support of his practice. Then one day she sent a very attractive girl to wait on him and told her to "vamp" him—if I may use the word popular in movies these days. I don't know how this Chinese vampire acted. Maybe she played her part like Norma Talmadge or maybe like Marie Prevost. But all to no avail. The monk continued sitting as still as a great mountain, eventually saying to the girl: "An old decayed tree grows in the cold rock. In the middle of winter it has no warmth at all." In plain American: "I am a piece of ice." So the girl told the old lady what he had said, upon which the old lady became so angry she drove the monk out of his lodging and burned his little house down!

Now what exactly was wrong with this monk? It goes without saying that he was not guilty of a single unchaste thought, word, or deed. He had not clung to anything in the world of impermanence. But he had seen only the negative side of his real I. He should not have neglected to share his Dharma with that little girl, no more than he should have refused it to the old lady.

We always say: this is good, that is bad; this is right, that is wrong. As far as judgment goes, this is all very well and good. But if you cannot give your audience some sense of true realization, what is the use of making all these noises?

Zen and Philosophy

(undated)

Generally speaking, I am a Buddhist, though I do not belong to any church or sect of Buddhism. As a citizen of the world, I have the right to study any teaching I choose to and to discuss any problem of human experience freely—just as in science and philosophy. I am sure you feel the same way.

Someone once asked: "Can any faith not based on the Christian Bible contain anything of value?" Fifty years ago—toward the end of the nineteenth century—this question would have been answered with a sharp and emphatic "No." That time has passed; the present age is an age of free thinking.

In philosophical terminology, Zen combines monism and pantheism. Some traces of pantheism—and polytheism too, for that matter—may be found in many Buddhist scriptures. The kind of pantheism in question I would call "materialistic" or just plain "atheistic." Buddhism is the backbone of Asian culture; and Zen is the soul of Buddhism.

Once a little girl and an adult were walking in a garden. The adult was reciting James Whitcomb Riley's poem "The Goblins Will Get You If You Don't Watch Out"—an uncanny freak of the imagination that is supposed to be attractive to children. The little girl said to him:

"But there isn't any such thing as a goblin and there isn't ever going to be any such thing!"

She was such a practical little girl! To which the adult replied:

"Maybe there isn't any such thing as anything."

Then she said to him, looking about the garden for something unquestionably real, "Yes, there is; there is such a thing as a squash."

Although there is such a thing as a squash, it is also true that there is no such thing as a squash separate from the whole universe. We just call a squash a squash; we could just as well call it an orange. Why not! Those who understand nothing but dualistic philosophy require the awakening Zen can provide. I wave my hand. But this is not really my hand. I clasp my hand; when I do so I am clasping the entire universe. And now, when I open my hand—there goes the entire universe! I am not trying to make things seem strange. I am just trying to show you the true absoluteness, oneness, or emptiness that lives vividly and flows eternally, the true absoluteness of Buddhism's Prajñāpāramitā.

Immanuel Kant referred to this absoluteness by the term "noumenon." They say in German, *"das Ding an sich,"* that is, "the thing in itself." In Kantian philosophy, noumenon is used to denote an object of thought which is not and cannot also be an object of intuition or perception, whether actual or possible. According to Kant, knowledge is possible only of objects of perception and is the result of the cooperation of conception—perception without conception being blind, and conception without perception, empty. Noumenon is an object of conception *period.* Here perception plays no part whatsoever. An example of such a pure object of conception would be what we call "soul" or "matter." In antithesis to noumenon is phenomenon. The little girl of our story accepted the phenomenon of squash, without realizing that the phenomenon of squash is not the real squash, does not represent what squash really is. The real squash is an object not of perception but of conception; the real squash is the noumenon squash, not the phenomenon of squash. To understand the noumenal aspect of squash requires a thinker's hard work. Zen will teach you how to realize the realm of noumenon in your daily life—one for all and all for one.[7]

Jalal-ud-din Rumi was a Persian philosopher and poet of the early thirteenth century. He was a Sufi thinker for whom the ego and the world and the divine were one. For him, God was the all-absorbing universe itself. This conception is quite reminiscent of the pantheism of the Vedanta, but Sufism has the virtue of having more poetic color to it. The Sufis look for their Beloved everywhere, so strongly devoted are they to Her. The Sufi's "experience in feeling God" or "way to the One" are but names for another gate through which to enter samādhi, that is, Zen meditation.

I am very much interested in the German mystics, especially Meister Eckhardt. He said: "The eye with which I see God is the eye with which God sees me." In Buddhism we say: "I come to the Buddha and the Buddha comes to me. Buddha, my mind, and all fellow beings are one." Eckhardt's pupil, Johann Tauler, preached what I would call a Christian pantheism that had much Zen in it. He was a fourteenth-century Dominican monk, who said: "Apart from God, there is no real thing." That was exactly Eckhardt's idea. Tauler went beyond Eckhardt and actually described the road leading to the truth. He called it *"die Welt in der Wüste,"* or "the world of wilderness." To be able to say something like this he must have seen the world before the first light appeared. Zen masters always say, "Show me your face before you were born." Tauler spoke of *Finsternis,* "the absolute darkness," and many a time spoke of *Abgrund,* "the bottomless abyss." Zen says: "You have nothing to receive and there is nothing to receive you. There is no space and no time; only one eternal now." Tauler must have experienced this condition of mind. His final conclusion was, *"Gott ist Nichts"*—God is nothingness. You see, he was able to enter Zen through a Christian gate. You can enter Zen through any gate—but you must not cling to any sect or doctrine; just walk freely and enjoy your emancipation. Then you will know that all teachings in the world are in reality your own inner treasure, all thoughts the running current of your own inner ocean.

The Japanese Zen master Sengai once wrote:

> What is Buddha?
> You may ask. Look at the weeping willow there!
> See the gesture of its thready limbs
>   playing with the breezes sweet!

Here is the whole thing—nothing more, nothing less. Here is the true intellectual oneness we seek, which can harmonize the respective claims of science and philosophy, poetry and religion. Here is also universal brotherhood, for as the Buddha said: "I see now, all beings have perfect wisdom and complete virtue. But they do not know it. I must show them the truth."

We ourselves must strive to find out what our true self is. Baha'i leader Abdul Baha said: "O people of the world, you are all the fruits of one tree and the leaves of one branch." Our friends who believe in Baha'ism would express these words in Esperanto as follows: *"Ho popolo de la mondo, vi estas ciuj la fruktoj de unu arbo kaj la folioj de unu branco."*

Reminiscence

(1934)

The fog was heavy in the mountains; the temple entirely enshrouded by it. Neither trees nor towers were visible. Everything seemed to have vanished. In this fog, as I ascended the stone steps one by one, I heard my master's voice far above me in the shrine. I had come to join him in his recitation of a chapter from the Sanskrit canon.

Every other day the lecture hall was open. My master's lectures were like constantly flowing streams. By following the current of his eloquence, we witnessed the great ocean of Dharma itself. The lecture over, he would enter into deep meditation, all of us joining him, like dull stars gathering about the brilliance of his North-Star wisdom.

Why were we secluded in this mountain temple? Nothing but realization was the reason. Some of us were sitting under old trees, others on moss-covered rocks as night spread its darkness around us without hesitation, dew falling heavily on our black robes. At midnight we entered our master's room one after another and received his personal guidance. Striking us with his stick and scolding us like a thunderstorm, he would remind us of what the Buddha had said: "I am the one who accomplished the meditation, and you are all presently on your way. Some day, everyone of you will become Buddha, just as I am now." Hearing this we smiled to ourselves, rejoicing after each stormy visit.

For the Dharma we consecrated our minds and bodies. Like the famous student of Bodhidharma,[8] we were even willing to cut off our arms and shed our blood upon the snow to express our stern devotion.

Sōyen Shaku passed away fifteen years ago. Though he no longer recites sūtras in his cell at Matsugaoka, anywhere and everywhere his eternal meditation continues. But now on moonlit nights in Kamakura, we hear only the familiar pealing of the ancient temple bell.

The Shapeless Tombstone[9]

(undated)

Emperor Daisō said to Echū, the National Teacher: "A hundred years from now you will be gone from the world. What sort of tombstone shall we make to remember you by?" Echū replied: "Just an ordinary tombstone will do." The emperor asked again: "What shape would you prefer?" The teacher kept silent for a while, and then asked: "Do you understand?" "No, I do not understand," answered the emperor. Echū said: "I am going to leave a disciple as my successor who knows about this matter. When the time comes, Your Majesty may ask him."

When the teacher had passed away, the emperor asked Echū's successor, Tangen, the same question. Tangen wrote this poem in response:

> South of the Shō, north of the Tan,
> Precious things pile up.
> In the country under the shadowless tree
> A ferry moors with all kinds of passengers.
> Across the water, the inhabitants of the jeweled palace
> Do not recognize each other.

Echū was the first National Teacher of Zen in China. The emperor Daisō reigned over China during the Tang Dynasty, from 765 to 779. This anecdote can be dated around 775, the year Echū passed away. He was a disciple of the Sixth Patriarch, Huineng. He had been hiding in a remote part of the mountains for forty years when the emperor discovered him and asked him to come forth to teach his subjects.

Echū must have been a very old man when he was asked about his tombstone. The emperor's "A hundred years from now…" is a polite way of referring to Echū's advanced age, since the Oriental convention is to consider the average age of a man to be one hundred.

Echū left a good disciple in Tangen. In his lineage there were many remarkable monks. Echū's life, therefore, was not lived in vain. The Shō and Tan were probably two rivers in the vicinity of the capital, but Tangen's reference is not really of a geographical nature. Anywhere Zen is, there Shō and Tan are also; any locality is Zen, and so is filled with "precious things." "Under the shadowless tree" means "timeless time," and "shadow" implies a reference to the sun and hence means "day." "A ferry moors with all kinds of passengers"—these are all bodhisattvas seeking truth, their destination being "across the water." "The jeweled palace" means utopia, where no one recognizes each other, each person carrying within himself his own independent ideal.[10] In this "palace" the terms "you," "I," "he," and "she" cease to obtain.

The poor emperor had in mind something like a big monastery or a huge tower. The teacher expressed his Zen by remaining silent, but the emperor—despite his crown—was unable to understand. He couldn't understand Tangen's poem either. This poem has become a kōan and is used in Zen practice. Since the time of this story, many Zen students have built tombstones for their teachers by becoming their own utopias.

Had I been Tangen, and had I been living in America, I would have expressed myself as follows:

> South of the Pacific, west of the Atlantic,
> The dormant oil is almost immeasurable.
> At the timeless station
> A train stops, with white and black passengers.
> In the White House of destination
> Capitalists and laborers are alike hatless.

Four Ways of Accepting Dharma

(1935)

There are four ways of accepting Dharma, or ultimate truth. One can accept the true meaning or spirit of the words in the sūtras, without clinging to the letter. One can accept the teaching with intuitive wisdom, without lingering in the world of cognition. One can accept only those sūtras which contain the highest teaching, without wasting time on those of lower grade. Finally, one can accept the teaching for the sake of the teaching, without attaching to the teacher himself. Let us discuss these four ways.

Although Buddhism first entered America some seventy years ago (around 1865), still only a very few people have been able to grasp its true meaning. Why do you suppose this is so? Because many students of Buddhism cling to the letter of the law in the sūtras. The best translations of sūtras were those done by enlightened monks, either those who came to India from China or to China from India. Not only were these translations done by enlightened monks, they were also supervised by masters who had attained the fruit of meditation.

A Chinese Buddhist scholar once said: "If you try to understand the true meaning of Buddhism by adhering to the letter, you are the enemy of the present Buddha, the past Buddhas, and all future Buddhas." Though they had the best translations, Chinese Buddhist students would still warn each other not to cling to the letter of the words. When studying sūtras, they would always meditate, so as to be able to free themselves from any attachment to merely literal interpretation.

So the first way to accept Dharma is by accepting the spirit rather than the letter of the words in the sūtras.

To illustrate the second way of accepting Dharma I will tell you a story (I am using D.T. Suzuki's translation):

Unmon was another great teacher of Zen at the end of the Tang Dynasty. He had to lose one of his legs in order to get an insight into the life-principle from which the whole universe takes rise, including his own humble existence. He had to visit his teacher Bokuju three times before he was admitted to see him.

The Master asked: "Who are you?" "I am Bunyen," answered the monk. (Bunyen was his real name, while "Unmon" was the name of the monastery where he was settled later on.) When the truth-seeking monk was allowed to go inside the gate, the Master took hold of him by the chest, and demanded: "Speak! Speak!"

Unmon hesitated, whereupon the Master pushed him out of the gate, saying "Oh, you good-for-nothing!" While the gate was hastily being shut, one of Unmon's legs was caught and broken. The intense pain resulting from this apparently awakened the poor fellow to the greatest fact of life. He was no more a solicitous, pity-begging monk; the realization now gained paid more than enough for the loss of his leg.[11]

This story makes it quite clear that the dualistic ideas characteristic of the world of cognition cannot lead one to true emancipation. I wish all of you to remember this second way of accepting Dharma: Accept the teaching with intuitive wisdom, without lingering in the world of cognition.

According to the Tendai school of Buddhism, the sūtras can be divided into eight parts, in accordance with a distinction between the form and nature of the teaching. Under the category of form are included the following: intuitive teaching, gradual teaching, esoteric teaching, and miscellaneous teaching. The category of the nature of the teaching comprises teaching for śrāvakas and pratyekabuddhas; teaching designed for these and for bodhisattvas as well; and teaching designed especially for bodhisattvas. The Nikāyas, or Pali texts, are gradual teaching for śrāvakas and pratyekabuddhas; the Mahāprajñā-pāramitā Sūtra, the Avatamsaka Sūtra, the Mahāparinirvāṇa Sūtra, and the Saddharma-Pundarīka Sūtra are esoteric and intuitive teaching designed exclusively for bodhisattvas. The rest of the sūtras are miscellaneous in nature; accordingly, these are suitable for so-called miscellaneous students.

Since our aim is to accept Dharma or ultimate truth, and not merely to be scholars of old scriptures, we should make a choice of those sūtras which contain the highest teaching, and not waste our time studying the others—except, of course, for reference purposes. The third way, then, is to accept those sūtras which belong to the highest teaching, without attaching to those of lower grade.

Non-Buddhist teachers from India, whether they be preachers of Brahmanism or Yoga, tend to emphasize mastership—especially in this country. Consequently, their students come to think that a master is someone superhuman, and practically worship their teachers. Strictly speaking, however, there is no such thing as a master in Buddhism. There are monks, nuns, upāsakas, and upāsikās. What is important is not some hierarchy, but the fact that we are all brothers and sisters trying to live a pure, unselfish Buddhist life. Elders may teach those younger than they; newcomers may receive instruction from older students. But since a saṅgha is a spiritual democracy which exists for the purpose of realizing a peaceful, harmonious way of life, there is no place in it for the kind of autocratic authority implied by the term "master."

If a man claims to be a master, he is no master at all. The master in Buddhism is like a rainbow—beautiful to look upon from afar, but vanishing when one sees it near at hand. We say: "Buddha is the best teacher; his teaching is conducive to true happiness; we are all in his brotherhood." So what need have we for a master?

In our faith, Buddha is our master and no one else. In our everyday activities, each of us is our own master of mind and body. When we engage in meditation, there is no objectivity, no subjectivity, no time, no space—and so no room for any master either! In conclusion: the fourth way to accept Dharma is to accept the teaching for the sake of the teaching, without attaching to the one who teaches.

Ageless Age[12]

(undated)

When Buddha announced that his death was imminent, one of his disciples asked him what to do with his relics. The Buddha said:

The bones and ashes from my cremated body will be taken care of by kings and men of the world. Let these people concern themselves with such things as the erection of pagodas and the building of temples to house my relics. Why should monks worry about the remains of my physical body, when the body of the Dharma—the excellent teaching of emancipation—will be with them always?

In keeping with this, his true disciples carried his Lamp of Dharma for generation after generation, transmitting its light to others. Kings and men of the world instead erected pagodas and temples to pay homage to his relics. In the course of time, these people began superstitiously worshipping the sacred remains themselves, for which they expected to receive much merit. Thus did Buddha's teaching become petrified—the exoteric doctrine as well as its esoteric substance.

In ninth-century China, during the Tang Dynasty, there was an emperor named Kensō, who devoted himself to the worship of Buddha's relics, which he thought would prolong his life, by virtue of some sort of miraculous power he believed them to possess. One of his subjects, a man named Kantaishi, a Confucian, appealed to the emperor to discontinue such worship, on the ground that all the ancestors of the Imperial Family had lived long lives without having had to resort to such superstition. The emperor was angered by his subject's opposition and exiled him from the capital. This crowned donkey knew about as much about Dharma as the Confucian did about Buddhism!

Near Kantaishi's house, where he lived in exile with his wife, there was a monastery. One day he paid a visit and met Daiten, the Zen master of the monastery. He asked the master, "How old are you?" Daiten held out his rosary and said, "Do you understand?" The exiled officer said, "No, I do not understand." Then the master said: "In the daytime, the beads of the rosary are 108; in the nighttime, the number is the same."

What the Confucian saw was only an old monk—hence his question. What the master showed him was the age of no beginning and no end.

Foolish Kantaishi was unable to see this at a glance, and so the master had to illustrate it for him. But it remained a puzzle and so Kantaishi returned home feeling quite displeased. When his wife asked him what had happened, he told her everything. The wife said: "That old monk seems to me a very kind-hearted person. I do not think he would puzzle you just for the fun of it. Why don't you ask him again to explain his meaning?"

Early the following morning, the henpecked husband returned to the monastery. At the gate he met the chief monk, who asked, "What makes you come here so early?" "I came to see your master," Kantaishi said. "What for?" "Well," said the Confucian, "yesterday I asked him his age and, saying nothing, he simply showed me his rosary. Of course I had no idea what he meant. Then he said something which I took as a joke and so I went home displeased. But my wife thought I should come back, so here I am. Do you know what your master meant?" The chief monk opened and closed his mouth three times, each time clacking his teeth together. Kantaishi could not understand the monk, either. When he finally met the master he asked, "What was the meaning of what you said yesterday?" Daiten opened his mouth three times, just as the chief monk had. The Confucian said: "I see now that Buddhism is the same everywhere." Daiten exclaimed, "How did you ever get such an idea!" Kantaishi replied, "I met your chief monk at the gate and asked him the same question, and he answered me in the same way." The master called for the chief monk and said, "I understand you preached Dharma to this man a few minutes ago. Is this true?" No sooner had the chief monk admitted he had by nodding than the master hit him with a big stick and expelled him from the monastery.

What do you make of this story?

The Confucian should not have transacted business with the chief monk that was meant for the master. Like a mother hen sitting on her egg, the Confucian should have carried his question to Daiten. This question was in fact his kōan, and from it could have come, if properly incubated, a lovely chick of realization. But the Confucian tried instead to solve his kōan through conventional means, and so it never hatched at all.

There is no way to prolong an individual life. Even someone who lives a hundred years must die sometime. When one realizes that one's true nature or inner self is Buddha-nature, he knows that he was never born and will never die. Although Kantaishi opposed the superstitious practice of the emperor—and was right in so doing—he himself was just as ignorant of Buddha-Dharma. He thought Buddha was merely some foreign god having nothing to do with the Chinese people. Had he acquired Zen from Daiten, he would have been able to understand the real meaning of the relics of Buddha, and to realize what Buddha's real relics are. Through such understanding he could have inspired not only himself and the emperor, but all the people of the kingdom.

The chief monk spoiled Daiten's game. He had no business intruding the way he did between student and master. He had probably attained his Zen by hearing the sound of Daiten's teeth. But to apply his own Zen to the case of the Confucian was as misguided as a hospital nurse giving the same medicine that cured her to another patient. The point here is not that Daiten wished to monopolize the Zen he had transmitted to the chief monk, but rather that the monk spoiled his teaching through its inappropriate application, and so had to be beaten and expelled.

A kōan is like medicine. In the hands of a doctor, it can cure; but in the hands of anyone else, it can poison and kill. The chief monk should have waited until he had a patient of his own to work on. All religions are afflicted with slavish imitation. Instead of creating new aspiration, disciples usually take the easy way out and merely do what others before them have done. The distinctions that exist among schools, sects, or denominations of religion exist only because of such slavish imitation. To avoid this I have tried to take off all the coverings or wrappers from my own teaching—"Buddhism," "Zen," "Sōtō," "Rinzai," "sect," "temple," "church"—and show you the bare truth, just as it is. Although the Buddha's words quoted at the beginning of this talk were addressed to monks, they apply to all Zen students. Anyone who has unnecessary wrappers, please take them off, without hesitation! When you do, you will know exactly how old Daiten is, and that we are all the same age: in the daytime, 108; in the nighttime, 108.

The Meaning of Sesshin

(1936)

Just as we do, Christians too have a self-denial week when they devote themselves to the faith and try to live an unselfish life. The Buddhist seclusion period has almost the same purpose and attitude behind it. We like to seclude ourselves at times from worldly affairs and stay in some solitary place to practice meditation. In Japan, Zen students call this *sesshin,* for which they normally set aside three, five, seven, or occasionally ten days. (The usual period of time is seven days.)

Sesshin has two meanings—since there are two Chinese characters, both having the same pronunciation. One meaning is "concentration of mind," the other, "unification of mind." In the first sense, "mind" has a psychological meaning. For example, when one reads a book and forgets one's surroundings, one is concentrating one's mind on that book. This is sesshin in the first sense. If our present seclusion were nothing more than this, we should all apologize to the occupants of this house for having temporarily deprived them of the comforts of their own home. Instead of bothering them for this sort of sesshin, we should have gone to a library or a park or garden!

In the second sense, "mind" means the essence of mind. It is this sort of sesshin we are concerned with. In Zen meditation we think nonthinking—that is, we think nothing. What this means is that our psychological mind ceases to function, and as a result, our whole being becomes united with the essence of mind, which we signify by "Mind." (You can call this essence "the God within you," "absoluteness," "Ultimate Reason"—it doesn't matter.) No matter what you call it, to unite with this essence is the very reason we are gathered here to meditate together.

For centuries philosophy and religion have tried to bring about this unification of mind, but without success. Zen will guide you there, as if you were returning to your long-lost home. In Zen meditation both heroic action and lifetime pleasure can be found. Someday, when you have attained your realization, you will appreciate the noble sacrifice this family has made so that we might hold sesshin together.

Professor Suzuki has written as follows about *shin* (*hsin* in modern Chinese), or "mind," in his *Manual of Zen Buddhism:*

Hsin is one of those Chinese words which defy translation. When the Indian scholars were trying to translate the Buddhist Sanskrit works into Chinese, they discovered that there were five classes of Sanskrit terms which could not be satisfactorily rendered into Chinese. We thus find in the Chinese Tripiṭaka such words as *Prajñā, Bodhi, Buddha, Nirvāṇa, Dhyāna, Bodhisattva,* etc., almost always untranslated; and they now appear in their original Sanskrit form among the technical Buddhist terminology. If we could leave *Hsin* with all its nuance of meaning in the translation, it would save us from many difficulties that face us in its English rendering. For *Hsin* means "mind," "heart," "soul," "spirit"—each singly as well as all inclusively. In Zen books it has sometimes an intellectual connotation, but at other times it can properly be done by "heart." But as the predominant note of Zen Buddhism is more intellectual than anything else, though not in the sense of being logical or philosophical, I decided here to translate *Hsin* by "mind" rather than by "heart," and by this mind I do not mean our psychological mind, but what may be called absolute mind, or Mind (with capital M).[13]

Though Suzuki has explained the matter well, still you might ask: Why didn't the Chinese simply create another character (to stand for this mind with a capital M)? I know I look like a Chinaman, but even so I cannot be held responsible for Chinese letters and characters! I can only say that the Chinese word *shin* (or *hsin*), having two meanings associated with it, is well suited actually to express the essence of Zen. Why? Because if there were two letters or characters, one for psychological mind, the other for absolute mind, the reader might think that there were in fact two different minds involved, each entirely alien to and separate from the other. Such a dualistic conception is the enemy of Zen! Your psychological mind moves like waves in the ocean; the ocean is the essence of mind itself. The mind that concentrates on the book is the very same Mind that embraces the whole universe.

During sesshin, we begin by concentrating our minds, but before long, as our meditation deepens, we find ourselves entering gracefully into the realm of samādhi where, without even knowing it, we realize the meaning of unification of mind.

The Three Treasures

(undated)

I would like to speak of the Three Treasures—Buddha, Dharma, and Saṅgha—from three points of view: the historical, the practical, and the philosophical.

The historical Buddha is Buddha Śākyamuni, the former prince Siddhartha; the historical Dharma, all Buddhist scriptures preserved since ancient times. The historical Saṅgha comprises all groups of Buddhist practitioners (monks, nuns, and laypeople) from the time of Buddha to the modern age.

If you cling too much to the historical Buddha, you will fall prey to the delusion of hero worship. If you depend too much on the historical Dharma—those old books that are really nothing but trash!—you may become blind to the brilliance of your own inner eye. And if you boast too much of the historical Saṅgha, you may become a churchgoer, a slave to convention, thereby disqualifying yourself from making any contribution whatsoever to the progressive current of world thought.

From the practical point of view, there have been many "small buddhas" (traditionally, *pratyekabuddhas*). Examples of these are Jesus Christ, Confucius, Plato, Socrates, Kant, Emerson, and many more. Their teachings are in turn examples of practical Dharma. For that matter, from this point of view, all schools of moral and philosophical teaching are practical Dharma treasures. Similarly, any group of friends, any society or circle of believers can be called a Saṅgha treasure in this practical sense.

The philosophical Buddha is none other than the whole universe. We speak here of Dharmakāya in Buddhism, or the Buddha's "true body." This idea corresponds to what is known as noumenon in Western philosophical terminology.

One of the meanings of Dharma is "phenomenon." From a philosophical point of view, noumenon and phenomenon are inseparable; and for this reason, Buddha (noumenon) and Dharma are also inseparable. Here is a simple example of what I mean: I sit in front of you and read this paper, while all of you sit still and listen to what I am reading. From a noumenal standpoint, I am not really here at all, nor are you really there. From a phenomenal point of view, things are as they appear—you are there and I am here. When we are able to go beyond my being here and your being there, when, that is, we are able to see ourselves in each other—when I can see you in me and when you can see me in you—then we will be able to realize the identity of noumenon and phenomenon, the identity of Buddha and Dharma.

The philosophical Saṅgha can be exhibited using this same example. When I can see you in me and you can see me in you, then, although each being-here and each being-there differs, nonetheless I can read my paper freely and you can listen freely and harmoniously, without your being-there being at all disturbed by my being-here. This is what Saṅgha means from a philosophical point of view.

When you attain your Zen—that is, when you acquire your own enlightenment—your mind will be just as clear as the mind of the historical Buddha; you will be one of the buddhas of the practical world. With your practical wisdom, you will see the waves and storms of phenomena as the Dharma of the practical world; and you will understand the historical Dharma as clearly as you would your own handwriting. Though we are living at present far from the time of Buddha Śākyamuni, when our everyday life becomes Saṅgha itself, then we realize the true meaning of Saṅgha. For this we must realize the essence of Dharma and the mystery of man and nature. This is the Zen way of attaining Triratna, or the Three Treasures, in this lifetime.

In Buddhism, everything is seen from three points of view: that of substance, of aspect, and of function. (These three points of view parallel Buddha, Dharma, and Saṅgha, as well as the philosophical, practical, and historical approaches to these Treasures.) For instance, I hold a pencil. The substance of this pencil is graphite and wood; its aspect is long and slender, somewhat like a chopstick in a Chinese restaurant. The function of this pencil is that of writing something on paper. Everything in this world—the Buddha included—can be seen from these three points of view.

The universe may also be seen from the standpoint of another three-fold classification: the three so-called "worlds" of desire, the material, and the nonmaterial. "God," "Brahma," or "Allah" all belong to the world of desire, since they are nothing but the postulations of human desire.

These three worlds constitute the substance of the universe. Just as there is nothing to be called the substance of this pencil except graphite and wood, so there is nothing in this universe apart from these worlds.

Sometimes we include in the substance of the universe something that is not classifiable in terms of these three worlds–something like "the soul," for example. The way this comes about is that we cling to a certain aspect of something and, in order to explain it, postulate some kind of substance existing outside of that aspect which, we presume, makes, rules, and governs it. In this way we arrive at the idea that there is such a thing as a soul, which is somehow responsible for mental and physical processes. Nonsense! We've never had such a thing, nor will we ever have such a thing!

Our body is nothing but a part of the material world, and our mind is nothing but a group of desires, a power of grasping in the world of desire. So-called "desire" is a function of the nonmaterial world. Because the material world is nothing but another form of the nonmaterial—a fact proven by modern science, which has shown that groups of matter are merely different groups of electrons, these in turn being nothing but a certain energy-form—our mind and body are not two different things, but just one substance with two aspects. Moreover, the same relation which obtains between your mind and your body obtains between your body and the whole universe—and between your mind and the minds of all sentient beings. So you see, the worlds of desire, of the material, and of the nonmaterial are one.

This sameness is absolute and infinite. To avoid the possibility of mis-understanding, however, we speak of this sameness negatively, calling it "nothingness" or "nirvāṇa." If you are enthusiastic about returning to your long-lost home, and if you strive in deep, constant meditation, all of you will attain realization and acquire nirvāṇa without fail. For the Buddha said: "Nirvāṇa is visible and present; inviting all to come and see; leading to the goal; intelligible to the wise; each for oneself."

An Evening of Zen with Dr. D.T. Suzuki

(Kawafuku Cafe, Los Angeles, December 20, 1936)

A Chinese dinner usually has no dessert course. But while you are enjoying your fruits, I would like to tell you what we are going to do this evening. We are spending an evening of Zen with Dr. Daisetz Teitarō Suzuki, whom we have already met and dined with as if members of the same fraternity. At dinner, there was no special seating arrangement, for as Einstein has said: "Each person is the center of the universe." Each person forgot his or her position, claim to fame, as well as other distinctions—even his or her own name, ideally! As it is with any Buddhist gathering, without having to introduce ourselves to each other, we all felt a congenial, mutual understanding, smiling at each other easily and without awkwardness. This is the way our evening of Zen began to unfold.

Now, what is Zen? If you have Zen in your life, you have no fear, no doubt, no unnecessary desires, and no extreme emotions. Neither illiberal thoughts nor egotistical actions trouble you. Serving humanity without thinking about it, you fulfill your presence in this world with loving-kindness, and are able to observe your own passing away as if it were nothing more than a petal falling from a flower. Thus you enter into that condition in which all sages dwell, enjoying life in blissful tranquillity.

"Zen" is the Japanized version of the Sanskrit *dhyāna*. Because the Chinese language has no phonetic letters, when Buddhism entered China translators had to use two Chinese characters to render as accurately as possible the pronunciation of this Sanskrit word. These characters at that time were pronounced "zen-na" (the modern Mandarin pronunciation would be "shan-na"). Because the lower character "na" is an auxiliary in Chinese grammar, it dropped off in the course of time, and the upper character "Zen" was considered the more important part of dhyāna (which means, roughly, "quietness," "meditation," or "contemplation"). Thus dhyāna entered Japan in the more simplified form of Zen.

Our Dr. Suzuki is the scholar-pioneer who transplanted Zen thought from the East to Europe and America. Zen is now growing rapidly among Occidental thinkers and, like the anglicized word "karma," will before long find its way into dictionaries, encyclopedias, and lexicons all over the world.

You see now what an evening of Zen with Dr. Suzuki means to American Zen students. Soon you will be able to hear from Dr. Suzuki himself what this Zen really is. In the meantime let us take an after-dinner break, say about ten minutes. Japanese hostesses will tell you where the smoking room is, so you can puff your Zen to your heart's content! Then this room will be purified by a Japanese archer. Watching what he does, you can catch a glimpse of bushido, but you may also see Zen itself, in the context of physical culture. Next there will be meditation. Just maintain your golden silence in your own way. A student who expresses his Zen with the flute will join us a few minutes before and after our meditation. Then Dr. Suzuki's lecture. Japanese music will follow his lecture, after which tea will be served. We do not speak of politics or economics in the tea room—that is not the Zen way! After tea, you may introduce yourself to Dr. Suzuki. I say all of this now, because if I were to insist on such things in the tea room, I would show I have no Zen!

I think Dr. Suzuki should know by now how to turn off questions from American ladies—after all, he married one! I bring this up because I do not want him to get too tired after his long trip. His wife, Beatrice Lane Suzuki, has written many books on Buddhism and Japanese culture. She is a well-known Buddhist writer of our day, and American Buddhists should be proud of her.

If I close the meeting sooner than you would like, please do not blame me. No one would like Dr. Suzuki to stay more than I. I studied Zen with him under the same teacher some forty years ago. Then after ten years had passed, I met him again in America. Now, thirty-one years later, I am with him once more. His boat leaves San Francisco on the twenty-fourth,

From left: Mihoko Okamura (D.T. Suzuki's secretary),
Nyogen Senzaki, D.T. Suzuki, Kangetsu Ruth McCandless. Japan 1955

but the condition of my health will not permit me to see him off. So, like good Buddhists, let us make this meeting a gathering both of welcome and farewell. Let us wish Dr. Suzuki bon voyage and a happy return to the land of Zen!

Three Pictured Fans
(comments on some of the Ten Oxherding Pictures)[14]

(1939)

The first *uta* (another name for a *waka*, a thirty-one syllable poem) is "Searching for the Ox." My translation is:

How and when it happened I do not know,

But my ox is gone!

Searching for the stray ox,

I am now entering into the remote mountains of meditation.

We recognize in ourselves the loss of something precious. This recognition evokes the Old Testament story of Paradise Lost. Christians blame the serpent's evil advice for Adam and Eve's expulsion from the Garden of Eden. But Buddhists blame nobody but themselves for their ignorance. Buddhists know it is their own lack of mindfulness that has caused the ox to stray. Every one of us is born with a wisdom that transcends all ideas and thoughts. This wisdom is symbolized in the Zen tradition by the ox. For the Buddhist, the Tree of Knowledge is the dualistic mind. However, since the ground of this mind is nondualistic, is Mind itself, the Buddhist has no reason to condemn eating of this tree's fruit, nor to blame dualism in general. Where it says in Genesis, "In sorrow shalt thou eat of it, all the days of thy life," Buddhism concurs—but with the significant qualification that if one succeeds in recovering one's lost wisdom, sorrow ceases to exist![15] How people can recover this wisdom, which will enable them to live happily in the world, is what is depicted in these beautiful pictured fans.

At the beginning stage of practice, you do not know how or when it happened, but you know your ox is gone, and feel a vague uneasiness at the thought of its absence. The deeper your grief becomes, the higher will your aspiration become. When your aspiration to recover your ox has been aroused, the pleasures of the six senses will no longer stay you; temptations of wealth and fame will no longer sway your mind. You will go onward, straightforwardly pursuing your lost ox. Step by step, the road of meditation will become more and more difficult. There will be rocky hills to be climbed over. Above the valley a perilous ledge awaits your attempt at passage. A dangerous wall of huge rocks and stones threatens you. But you fear nothing, simply marching on bravely, thinking neither of past, present, nor future, searching for your ox in an eternal present. Actually to experience this stage of meditation is immediately to enter into the remote mountains of dhyāna. Then you are a true Zen student, a hero of Zen. Having passed the first kōan in the Oxherding Series, you can dry your sweat with the first fan.

The second *uta* is "Seeing the Traces." My translation goes:

> Many a time I searched for the ox
> And wandered in the mountains.
> At last I discovered the traces of the hoofs
> Impressed here and there!

Not many people search for the ox. Among those who do, only a fortunate few even discover its traces. In books or in actual life, we may discover such impressions of the ox, but often we confuse these with traces of another sort. Many students wander for years without seeing even traces of wisdom.

In Rabindranath Tagore's translation of *The Songs of Kabir* we read:

> O servant, where dost thou seek me?
> Lo! I am beside thee.
> I am neither in the temple nor in the mosque.
> I am neither in Kaaba nor in Kailash.
> Neither am I in rites and ceremonies, nor in Yoga
>   and renunciation.
> If thou art a true seeker, thou shalt at once see me.
> Thou shalt meet me in a moment's time.

Constant meditation gives one watchful eyes, ever ready to catch a glimpse of the traces of truth. When the time comes—with such eyes—one cannot fail to perceive, not only impressions of the ox, but the ox itself.

The third *uta* is:

> At a spot in the spring field
> Where the thready willow invited me
> I discovered my long-lost ox!

As with receiving tea, so with self-realization: you hold your empty cup, you are ready; but you must wait for someone to pour the tea. Self-realization, or bumping-squarely-into-your-true-self, usually involves a so-called "karma-relation" (an uncanny coincidence, a trigger, or mysterious connection that can't be rationally explained), in the same way that drinking tea usually involves its being poured by someone.

At the stage expressed by this third *uta,* one's meditation is mature. There is neither relativity nor absoluteness. You are now far above both sameness and difference. You have nothing to receive and there is nothing to receive you. There is no time—no space—just one eternal "now." The person in this uta had already entered into this condition of readiness, but was still unable to attain realization, until coming upon the weeping willow in the field. On the verge of their awakening, some hear the sound of a temple bell; some glance at a cloud in the sky. These are examples of karma-relation. Some monks pass their kōans under their master's beating whip; some attain it while washing their faces in the morning. No matter how hard you try, however, you cannot find the karma-relation that will enlighten you by looking for it. Instead of seeking out your karma-relation, devote yourself to constant meditation, with no desire for attainment. Then the doors of the gateless gate will open for you by themselves.

Each of us should strive to be the master of our own mind and body; to govern our environment in a peaceful manner; to lead a pure and unselfish life; and to be kind and helpful to our fellow beings. *These* are our important tasks.

Book of Equanimity, Chapter Three: Prajñādhāra Recites His Sūtra[16]

(1944)

BANSHŌ'S INTRODUCTION

Monks, go back to the timeless era. There you can see the black turtle run toward the fire and hear the voice of the wordless teaching. Can you recognize the flowers blossoming on the millstone? What kind of scripture will you recite in that region?

SENZAKI'S COMMENT

Banshō here raises the curtain on that vivid stage where buddhas and ancestral teachers perform their best acts. Western scholars who criticize Buddhism, but are themselves without Zen experience, may be found hooting from their seats under the advertising curtain. Hermann Minkowski states:

> Henceforth, Space in itself and Time in itself sink into mere shadows and only a kind of union of the two can be maintained as self-existent.

We postulate something called "tomorrow" and think of it as a duration separated from "today." But when tomorrow comes, it turns out to be today; and so one postulates another tomorrow, which is nothing but an extension of that tomorrow and this today, and so on, endlessly. We worry about a so-called "hereafter," but our own individual death is not the end of the world! This hereafter is not what we think it is. For example: My present life is the hereafter for someone else who died before me, and in this present life I unwittingly carry on the work of someone else, just as someone else will without question carry on my work after I have died. So why worry about one's own little death! The world is timeless.

Past, present, and future are merely names that refer back to the relative perspective these conventions presuppose.

An ancient philosopher once visited the tyrant of Syracuse in Sicily. The tyrant told him all about his plans for the future, his schemes and projected conquests, and finally said to the philosopher: "After all of this has been accomplished, after I have built a city, declared war on Messina, as well as on other countries, and have conquered them all, then I shall settle down and be happy." The philosopher said, "Why don't you settle down now and be happy?"

Those who do not know the region of the timeless that Banshō is pointing to in his introduction, always blame others for their own misdeeds and never examine themselves; they are thus condemned to engaging in endless conflict.

In China the black turtle lives in the deep sea, only sometimes coming out of the water to wander onto land. Using his instinct, sooner or later he goes back to the sea. When Banshō speaks of the black turtle's approaching fire instead of water, it is his way of crushing prejudice and *Ideologie*.[17] When he asks, "Can you recognize the flowers blossoming on the millstone?" the reader is being invited to loosen his tight hold on conventional ideas (since flowers do not blossom on millstones!). "The wordless teaching" transcends the music of notes and technique.

Birds are flying creatures, but ostriches, cassowaries, and emus in Australia, as well as kiwis in New Zealand and penguins in Antarctica, cannot fly at all. Fish live in water, but the climbing perch climbs trees (and sideways at that!), flapping its way up to a height sometimes of five feet or more. On the shores of the Bay of Stilis in Greece there are goats that have the peculiar habit of building large nests in trees. If you ask a child, "Why is a pig so dirty?" you will get the reply: "Because it's a pig!" "A Jap is a Jap" and "A Jew is a Jew" are similar examples of this kind of simpleminded prejudice and *Ideologie*.

Banshō's monks thought it their business to recite sūtras before accepting food, just as Christian ministers pray before dining. This clinging to conventions should have been crushed by the time they reached the theme of this chapter.

MAIN SUBJECT (selected by Zen Master Wanshi)

A king of eastern India invited Prajñādhāra, the teacher of Bodhidharma, to a royal feast, expecting to get a recitation of some kind out of this learned monk. Prajñādhāra, after having remained silent for a while, began to eat. The king asked, "Why don't you recite the sūtras?" The monk replied: "My inhalation does not tangle itself up with the five skandhas; my exhalation goes out freely without becoming ensnared in the chain of cause and effect. Thus I recite a million scrolls of holy scripture."

SENZAKI'S COMMENT

Buddha Sākyamuni used to call his preaching "turning the Wheel of Dharma." Just like the ancient Indian wheel-weapon capable of sweeping the enemy off its feet, so the Buddha's teaching was capable of completely crushing the delusions of humankind. The spiritual medicine prescribed was always in accordance with the particular sickness to be cured. Buddha's teachings were transmitted verbally from teacher to student, from mouth to ear. The sūtras, or holy scriptures, were thus recited by disciples in their original form—Sanskrit or Pali, and, later, in Chinese translations. To recite scriptures without knowing the true meaning of the teaching they contain is like murmuring the pharmacopoeia without having examined the patient! The king in this kōan was foolish enough to expect to get—in return for his royal feast—some magical words from the Patriarch, as well as the merit deriving from having fed such a "holy man." Wanshi's and Banshō's monks thought they were followers of the Buddha just because they could recite sūtras. It was to combat this clinging to the conventional that the present chapter was written.

The five skandhas are: *rūpa* (form), *vedana* (sense perception), *samjñā* (thought), *samskara* (discrimination/volition), and *vijñāna* (consciousness). These are the processes through which mind and body, the inner and the outer, the subjective and the objective, interweave. Because Prajñādhāra is able to breathe in and out without becoming entangled in the five skandhas, he transcends the suffering which is the necessary consequence of attachment to these constituents of consciousness. It was from this same condition of karma-free samādhi that the Buddha himself started turning his Wheel of Dharma. And this condition is the source of all the sūtras, or holy scriptures, of Buddhism.

Dōgen Zenji tells us, "In your meditation you should think nonthinking. Now what is nonthinking? It is to think nothing."

A well-known Japanese actor was asked by his understudy: "How is it you say your part on opening night as if you'd already performed it many times?" To which the actor responded: "I first practice it many times in rehearsal, but then try to forget it completely the night before the first performance."

Kōans are usually solved when one is not meditating. In true meditation there is nothing to think about—even one's kōan should be forgotten. The purpose of kōan study is to drive the student into this region of nothingness.

VERSE (composed by Zen Master Wanshi)

> The rhinoceros takes his walk in the moonlight.
> The wooden horse plays with the spring breeze.
> A pair of cold, blue eyes
> Glares behind the white bushy eyebrows.
> He does not read sūtras with those eyes.
> His mind extends into the timeless region.
> No victory without struggle.
> The perfect machine moves with one touch.

Kanzan forgets his way home;
Jittoku returns with him, hand in hand.

SENZAKI'S COMMENT

The rhinoceros walks under the moon; no one knows what he wants; he is neither hungry nor thirsty. The Chinese call him "a desireless walker." The wooden horse enjoys his freedom—no one can tie him up. The Patriarch lives the same unconcerned life as these two. To reach this stage, however, requires very hard work, a constant battle against the inertia of delusion. (Kanzan is the manifestation of Mañjuśrī, or enlightenment; Jittoku of Samantabhadra, or loving-kindness.)

Esoteric Buddhism

(undated)

The Japanese Zen master Dōgen once said: "Everyday life is a noble life. The body which maintains this life is a noble body. Do not waste your life. Do not neglect your body. Respect the body and adore this life."

Some of you may think that because Buddhism speaks of the transitoriness of things, it does not believe life has any real value. But on the contrary, more advanced students of Buddhism know that this very body is the body of the Buddha; this very mind, the Buddha-mind itself. These students, following the words of Dōgen, respect their bodies and minds accordingly. It is only negative Buddhism that denies so-called "self-nature"; positive Buddhism acknowledges a self-nature that is none other than the eternal, selfsame body of the Buddha.

A monk once asked Jōshū: "Master, I have nothing in my mind. Would you call this enlightenment?"

Jōshū said: "Throw it out!"

To this the monk replied: "But if I have nothing in my mind, what shall I throw out?"

Jōshū said: "If you won't throw it out, then you'll have to carry it with you."

The monk was immediately enlightened.

Though his mind was clear, this monk at the outset was still clinging to the idea of clearness, and it was for this reason that Jōshū told him to clear this idea out as well. The monk who came to Jōshū had a spotless mind—as bright as a mirror—but he lingered in that brightness, not unlike a student of the Vedanta. Jōshū wanted to break that mirror in order to show him what real freedom is. In acting the way he did, he was like a good mother who tells her son not to take his medicine but be sick in bed as long as he likes! This story helps us break the habit of becoming entangled in words.

To the Western mind, the doctrine of the nonexistence of the soul is a doctrine of despair. When American scholars hear of the selfsame, eternal body of the Buddha, they think they are hearing something from the Vedanta philosophy. Why? Western students have a tendency to look at statements superficially, without the third eye of inner wisdom. It is this inner wisdom which is known as "esoteric teaching" in the West. This is a misnomer; the proper expression is "esoteric *Buddhism*," and it is this school of Buddhism which is the subject of this talk.

"Esoteric Buddhism" means that the essence of Buddhism is beyond words and descriptions. It cannot be understood through any psychological analysis of mental processes; nor by epistemological investigations of the process of cognition; nor by philosophical generalization. Words are empty shells; they are incapable of conveying essence. In speaking to you about esoteric Buddhism, I hope to do something beyond words and descriptions—to encourage you all to seek out the brilliance of your own inner wisdom by yourself.

Some think of esoteric teaching in terms of mysteries and miracles, awaiting with keen interest manifestations of supernatural power entirely free from the law of causation! Such an expectation is nothing but superstition; and one who has not freed oneself from this kind of ignorance is not yet ready to study Buddhism.

Others think the transmission of esoteric teaching can only be done by a master. If by "master" they mean an actual flesh-and-blood person, they are right; but if they mean "living Buddha" or some such superstitious idea, they are still back with their irrational attachment to mysteries and miracles. So long as one fools around with such nonsense, one is not worthy of Buddha Sākyamuni's teaching!

The Japanese Buddhist sect called Shingon is based on esoteric teaching. I was ordained as a Buddhist monk under a Shingon teacher, and studied the Avatamsaka Sūtra. Later I entered a Zen monastery, where I studied meditation. Buddha used to tell his disciples that the knowledge which can be obtained in this life is like foliage in the hand; that which lies beyond our grasp is like all the foliage in the forest. For this reason I consider myself a mere infant in Buddha Sākyamuni's kindergarten, and am happy to have no sect name to apply to the Buddhism I live from day to day. I have never tried to convert any of my friends to any particular form of religion. I wish them only to enjoy their own emancipation.

Before introducing this Shingon teaching to you, I must remind you that every sect or religion has an inner gate, and that the distinction between the esoteric and the exoteric applies not only to Buddhism but to any religion, even Christianity. In Islam, for example, Sufism is the inner gate; and Inayat Khan, a modern Sufi master, has said of this inner gate: "The inner life is not necessarily opposed to the worldly life. It is only that the inner is a fuller life. Worldly life means the limitedness of life; the inner life is a complete life." This is just what the essence of Shingon is all about. Expressed in more traditional terms, Shingon is contained in these words: "I come to Buddha and Buddha comes to me. Buddha, my mind, and all fellow beings are one."

According to Shingon teaching, all things are complete in and of themselves, and as such are to be regarded as objective manifestations in our everyday life of Buddhist truth. That is to say—everything is Buddha.

I am sure you have seen Tibetan pictures depicting hundreds of Buddhas arranged like a sheet of postage stamps. This kind of picture is called a *mandala,* meaning "completeness" or "the whole." A mandala is a representation of the universe from which nothing has been excluded. The so-called "mandala of objectivity" is known as *garbha-kośa-dhātu* in Sanskrit, and *taizokai* in Japanese. Both the Sanskrit and the Japanese terms connote a pregnant state, as within a mother's body. In Shingon meditation the student faces one of these pictures and tries to unite with the universe, sitting cross-legged and thinking oneness, concentrating on the mandala while constantly repeating a formula known as a *dhāraṇī*. In the process of doing this, the world of objectivity becomes his own world—thatness melts away into thisness. At the point at which this takes place, thatness and thisness both give way to suchness—the self-existent, creative, and universal principle moving endlessly from eternity to eternity. Shingon's personification of this principle is known as Mahāvairocana.

In addition to the mandala of objectivity, there is the so-called "mandala of subjectivity." Shingon teaches that our senses, thoughts, desires, and delusions are all buddhas, each one being, because complete in itself, a complete exemplification of the wholeness of the universe. The mandala of subjectivity is known as *vajradhātu* in Sanskrit, and *kongōkai* in Japanese—the "diamond cutter," symbol of the power of wisdom to crush all delusion.

Shingon teaching makes use of so many symbols one needs a special dictionary to keep track of all of them. Because the purpose of this talk is to get a real taste of esoteric teaching—not to memorize names and symbols—let us consider rather how the Shingon theory can be put into practice.

To help us I shall quote from Rinzai Zenji, the famous Zen master of ninth-century China. Rinzai once said:

> My Zen works in four ways. First, I shut off my subjective world, accepting the objective world as it is. Second, I shut off the objective world, living alone in my subjective world. Third, I shut off both subjective and objective worlds, living in nothingness. Fourth, I open up my subjective world and enter freely into the objective world.

Let us see how this Zen can be practiced, and how such practice is related to the Shingon teaching. According to the Bible, when Jesus was crucified he cried out, *"Eli, Eli, Lama Sabachthani"*—"My God, My God, why hast Thou forsaken me!" Applying Rinzai's four ways, we may say that Jesus had shut off the subjective world and was squarely facing the objective world.

In the second stage you shut off the objective world, and live alone in your subjective world. The only way, after all, to get anywhere is to start from where you are. You are the center of the universe, the master of your fate. Once you shut off thatness, eternal thisness remains.

In the third stage, you shut off both the objective and the subjective worlds. Two mirrors now stand face to face, reflecting nothing but each other. Because they use too many figures and objects in their meditation, modern Shingon students never reach this stage. But this is the palace of meditation; here thisness and thatness melt into absolute nothingness. You are forbidden, however, to linger here too long. You must move on, move on!

We come at last to the fourth stage. You open both your objective and your subjective world. You see the beautiful interwovenness of thatness and thisness. The struggle of your life becomes your paradise, and you enjoy your work, no matter what you are doing.

This is what Shingon teaching aims at; but in the absence of the right sort of experience and striving, Shingon students will never be able to enter this inner shrine. Merely believing you are buddha from the very beginning will not further you along the Buddhist path. What is most essential is the keeping of the moral precepts and the living of a pure, unselfish life. Otherwise—Shingon or no Shingon—you will have nothing but suffering in this world, and will remain in the darkness of ignorance—until and unless you really get sick and tired of it!

Master Tōrei prescribed rules and regulations governing activities in his meditation hall. I would like to translate and read some of them to you, and so end this talk. I have chosen those I thought would be most worthwhile for our American friends who are eager to attain esoteric wisdom.

First: We gather here to study meditation and nothing else. Even a stranger will be accepted warmly, if you are sincere and earnest in seeking Buddha-Dharma, the universal truth. No matter how well known to the world you may be, you will not be allowed to enter the meditation hall unless you prove yourself to be a worthy disciple of Buddha, the Enlightened One. We associate with many people in the course of our everyday life, people from all walks of life, but the interior of this meditation hall is our consecrated holy place, and no one but true Zen students will be allowed to enter. Even though you may be our intimate friend, if you who seek entrance are not pure of purpose, we will shut the door in your face—without hesitation.

Second: This teaching is like climbing a mountain. The more you advance, the more you have to climb. Until you reach the summit you will not be able to see Buddha-Dharma, or universal truth, as it really is, in its full entirety.

Third: The Palace of Meditation is in the Sea of your Mind. The more you research, the more you must enter deeper and deeper—until you reach the bottom, you will not be able to obtain the hidden treasure of prajñā, the supreme knowledge of Buddhism.

The Diamond Sūtra

(San Diego, May 19, 1946)

Fellow Students: This evening I am going to speak on the Diamond Sūtra, a Buddhist scripture which we Zen students often use. The Diamond Sūtra was introduced to the West for the first time by Csoma Korosi in 1836. He wrote an outline of the sūtra in an English periodical, *Asiatic Researches.* The source of his paper was the Tibetan translation of the sūtra. In the next year, 1837, a German scholar, a man named Schmidt, translated the entire sūtra into German and published it in Russia. Samuel Beal, in 1865, translated the Diamond Sūtra from the Chinese into English. Max Müller, in 1881, published the original Sanskrit text, and, in 1894, he also published this English translation in *The Sacred Books of the East,* volume 49. My friend Dr. Dwight Goddard published his work on the sūtra, but rearranged the chapters. He referred to the translation of Gimmel, who had used the Chinese text. I usually use Dr. Suzuki's translation in his *Manual of Zen Buddhism,* even though it is abridged and has only twenty-one of the thirty-two chapters of the original Chinese.

This sūtra was brought to China by Kumārajīva, in the beginning of the fifth century. There were seven different translations before the middle of the seventh century, but I consider the translation of Kumārajīva the best among them. I have here with me that Chinese text. I use it for my everyday chanting.

Many commentaries on this sūtra have been written, both in Chinese and in Japanese—probably adding up to three hundred books or more. Further details concerning bibliographic descriptions will hardly give you even a glimpse of the sūtra, so I will tell you an anecdote:

A monk was doing zazen in the library of a monastery. The librarian came to him and asked him why he was doing zazen, rather than reading books. The monk said, "I am looking for commentaries on the Diamond Sūtra."

The librarian brought him ten or twelve books which treat the sūtra. The monk did not look at them, but kept on doing zazen. After a little while the librarian came to the monk again and said, "Well, brother, did you learn something about the Diamond Sūtra? If you have some difficulty in reading the books I will be very glad to help you."

The monk stood to his full height and said, "No, thank you. This is what I was looking for."

The librarian could not understand the monk at all. What the monk showed him was too simple and too deep. You see, the great elephant does not walk on the rabbit's playground. Supreme enlightenment goes beyond the narrow range of book learning.

I have here a commentary on the Diamond Sūtra which is, I think, the best of all commentaries. It is hidden in these Buddhist beads. Those who wish to read it, step inside any bead and study it to your heart's content! I am not talking of some sort of magic or miracle. I am not going to monopolize this particular commentary by myself. Any one of you can enter into a marble or a bead, if you learn how to do it. It does not matter whether you are stout or slender. Some day you will do it easily and freely in the same graceful manner as you entered into this room. Then you will read the best of all commentaries of the Diamond Sūtra at a glance—nay, you will be graduated from the whole course of the teaching which the Diamond Sūtra discloses.

The Sanskrit name of the Diamond Sūtra is Vajracchedika-Prajñā-pāramitā Sūtra. *Prajñā* is wisdom, and *pāramitā* means to enlighten oneself in order to enlighten others. We Buddhists aim to attain enlightenment, to make others happy. We do not consider our own pleasure of attainment, but simply strive to serve all sentient begins. *Prajñāpāramitā* therefore is the wisdom of the bodhisattvas, whose motives and constant work are altruistic.

These days, we see many teachers whose motives are to have rank and to dominate others. If a student of such so-called spiritual teachers attains the same wisdom as the teacher, it makes that teacher unhappy. The teacher has egotistically collected his knowledge to sell to others for a good price—perhaps not visible, materialistic gain, but more likely fame or glory among his followers. Such cannot be compared with *prajñā-pāramitā*.

The wisdom of the bodhisattvas was named by Buddha *vajracchedika,* the pulverizer of all delusions. It cuts as a diamond cuts a windowpane. It is as rare as the diamond is among other jewels. It is as beautiful as the polished diamond.

Sūtra is the scripture, and like this string of Buddhist beads, it holds together the sayings of Buddha. Now you understand the name Vajracchedika-Prajñāpāramitā Sūtra.

This sūtra teaches us egolessness, formlessness, nondwelling, and nonattainment. We have no entity within us to be called ego. We only postulate our desires and call that ego. Everything appears as if it exists, but we only recognize things in relative terms. The world is formless—simply a phenomenon of flux, consisting of various relations, conceivable only in relation to subjectivity and objectivity. Without this close relation, there is no thing, there is no world. Nondwelling means nonattachment. Nonattachment discourages our clinging ideas of loss and gain.

A Japanese mother wrote the following letter to her son, Jiun, a great scholar and lecturer of Sanskrit, Shingon, and Zen in the Tokugawa era (1603–1867):

> Son, I do not think you have become a devotee of Buddha because you wished to become a walking dictionary for others. There is no end to information and commentaries, glory and honor. I wish you would stop this lecture business. Shut yourself up in a little temple in a remote part of the mountains and devote your time to zazen! In this way you will attain true realization.

Jiun's mother was declaring the idea of nondwelling from her understanding of the Diamond Sūtra.

Some Americans go to Asian countries and pick up a few items of information from the natives. On the very day of their arrival home, they want to teach others something of that culture. They should read this letter of Jiun's mother before they start such a bargain sale. Whoever thinks that he or she has attained enlightenment is losing it at that moment. Those who claim themselves to be masters or saints are merely exposing their ignorance. Do not be cheated by them! Use the Diamond Sūtra as an acid test and see whether they are speaking and acting according to this teaching.

In early times in Japan, people used bamboo and paper lanterns with candles inside. A blind man was visiting a friend one night. He was offered a lantern to carry home with him. "I do not need a lantern," he said. "Darkness and light are all the same to me."

"I know you do not need a lantern to find your way," his friend replied, "but if you don't have one, someone else may run into you, so you must take it."

The blind man started off with the lantern and before he had walked very far, someone ran squarely into him. "Look where you are going!" he exclaimed to the stranger. "Can't you see this lantern?"

"Lantern? How could I know? Your candle has burned out," replied the stranger.

Subhūti was the disciple for whom Buddha preached his Diamond Sūtra. He was able to understand the potency of emptiness, the viewpoint that nothing exists except in the relationship of subjectivity and objectivity. One day Subhūti, in a mood of sublime emptiness, was sitting under a tree. Flowers began to fall about him. "We are praising you for your discourse on emptiness," the gods whispered to him.

"But I have not spoken of emptiness," Subhūti said.

"You have not spoken of emptiness. We have not heard of emptiness," responded the gods. "This is true emptiness."

And blossoms showered upon Subhūti like rain.

Now I will read from chapters twenty-eight and twenty-nine of the Diamond Sūtra, as it appears in the *Manual of Zen Buddhism.*

> Then the Buddha uttered this gātha:
> "If anyone by form sees me
> By voice seeks me
> This one walks the false path
> And cannot see the Tathāgata."

> Again Buddha said to Subhūti: "Subhūti, if a man should declare that the Tathāgata is the one who comes or goes, or sits, or lies down, he does not understand the meaning of my teaching. Why? The Tathāgata does not come from anywhere, and does not depart to anywhere; therefore, he is called the Tathāgata."

Ripe, Unripe Fruit

(undated)

Confucius said: "There are three friendships which are advantageous, and three which are injurious. Friendship with the upright, with the discerning, and with the sincere—these are advantageous; friendship with the man of specious airs, with the insinuatingly soft, and with the glib-tongued—these are injurious." A Buddhist Saṅgha is a group of friends whose friendships are advantageous, in the sense Confucius has so well defined. I am thankful for the privilege of being one of these Saṅgha friends, and for being able to keep myself free from injurious friendships.

As the good old Buddhist Shinran said: "I am not a teacher, but a member of this group of harmonious friends. I have neither disciples nor pupils of my own." Buddhist monks have no concept of home, but when good friends like you gather around me, I begin to feel as if I had indeed found a home. Like Hotei-san, I am a very happy monk. Have you ever seen a statue of a fat Chinese monk carrying a linen sack and smiling happily? In Chinatown the storekeepers call him the Happy Chinaman. That is Hotei-san. Someday I will tell you more about him. Actually, since you're talking right now to one of his cousins, you really don't need to hear much more! Instead, I will tell you a few stories about some other Chinese monks.

Whenever the great master Baso was asked, "What is Buddha?" he would reply: "That mind of yours is Buddha." If you ask me, I will make the same reply. Baso's answer should not be interpreted as some kind of philosophical idealism, however. He is not saying that the Buddha has no real existence; that it exists only in your mind. You have no mind you can claim as your own anyway! The reality of the Buddha could not derive from the reality of your mind, since in fact there is no such reality. What is your mind? It is not sensation, it is not perception, it is not consciousness—it is not any of the constituents associated with it. So when Baso said, "That mind of yours is Buddha," what could he have meant? What did he really mean? This is your kōan, or theme for meditation. The other day I wrote an *uta;* I will translate it for you into English:

> What is Buddha?
> You should have looked before you asked.

Although Baso answered, "That mind of yours is Buddha," no matter what the question or who the questioner, he was not one of those modern ministers who give the same canned—almost playful—response, "God is Love," no matter what they are asked. The difference is that with his words Baso was able to open the heart of anyone who questioned him; he was able actually and directly to touch the hinges of that person's mind. And, like a good sculptor, he did not need many tools.

Eighty masters were produced from among Baso's disciples. One of these was called Daibai. Upon having heard his master's words, Daibai put off his heavy burdens and retired to live in the mountains for many years, where he could enjoy and deepen his attainment. Like a true scholar, Daibai was in no hurry to market his knowledge or wisdom. Zen masters used to hide themselves in remote parts of the world, meditating in the deep mountains among trees and rocks, with monkeys and rabbits for companions. They did so not because they were misanthropic, but because they wanted to guard their Dharma against the dust of glory and fame. Modern students of religion are altogether too impatient. Without waiting for the fruit to ripen, they open up their stores and begin to sell their wares. Such unripened fruit is unhealthy, and may cause injury to those who do not know the difference.

Daibai was not one of these quick sellers. One day in the mountains a friend from his old monastery found him and was asked by Daibai: "What answer does our master give these days when asked 'What is Buddha'?" The visitor said: "Our teacher changed his answer recently. Now he says, 'That mind of yours is not Buddha.'" To this Daibai replied: "No matter what my old teacher says, I say: 'This mind of mine is Buddha.'" I want all of you to think this one over.

The visiting monk returned to the monastery and told Baso what Daibai had said. Then Baso remarked: "I see now that big fruit has ripened." He must have been very pleased indeed to have uttered such admiring words.

Afterward, a monk asked Baso why he had begun saying, "That mind of yours is Buddha" in the first place. Baso said: "I wanted the children to stop their crying." The questioner continued:

"When the children had stopped their crying, what would you say then?"

Baso answered: "That mind of yours is not Buddha."

"Suppose one neither cries nor wishes candy, then what would you say?"

The master rejoined: "There is nothing."

The questioner then asked: "If there were someone who neither cried, nor needed candy, nor clung to nothingness, what would you propose to him?"

The master replied: "Such a person would be a master already and could handle all situations by himself. What would I have to say to him!"

When Baso was very sick and nearing death, an attendant, greatly concerned, asked him how he felt. "Sun-faced Buddha, Moon-faced Buddha," was the reply. It is said that the Sun-faced Buddha lives for 1,800 years, the Moon-faced Buddha only one night. So Baso was saying: "Some buddhas have lived for one thousand eight hundred years, and some for only one night. What difference does it make if I die tomorrow?" Now while I certainly don't want any of you to die before you are very old, I do want you all to die like buddhas—peacefully and calmly. We are performing birth-and-death every minute, every hour, every day and every year. Whether you make yourself a three-minute Buddha or a ten-year Buddha is up to you. Only two more days remain of this seclusion week. Make yourselves at least two-day buddhas!

Buddha's Birthday Celebration

(April 11, 1948)

Bodhisattvas: This is the celebration of Buddha's birthday, and your congenial spirit of gladness, such as you are expressing today, is the most beautiful decoration in this humble Buddhist home.

If you were in Japan in the month of April, you would see the celebration of Buddha's birthday observed everywhere. To the people of Japan, the eighth of April, Buddha's birthday, is like Easter Sunday to Americans. The spirit of resurrection, the blessedness of eternity, and the sensibility of rejuvenation are almost the same there as here. As for Buddha, he is no longer a teacher of only Eastern adherents. Now he is one of the great teachers of the world.

According to the sūtras, Queen Maya dreamed one night that she saw a star in the heavens, with shining rays of six different colors. Underneath the star, a white elephant with six tusks appeared and walked toward her. This queen was living in the city of Kapilavasthu, in the Śākya kingdom of India, with her king, Śuddhodana, who belonged to the royal family of Gautama. She was as beautiful as the water lily and as pure in mind as the lotus.

Next morning, the queen summoned the official seer, and asked him to interpret her dream. The seer said, "You are destined to become the mother of the greatest and noblest sage."

When she knew that the time of motherhood was near, she asked the king to send her to the palace of her parents, as this was the custom in India for the first-born child. The king granted her request willingly and sent her to the neighboring city with a royal cortege.

When the queen passed the garden of Lumbinī, the trees were a mass of fragrant flowers and many birds were warbling in their branches. Wishing to stroll through the shady walks, she left her golden palanquin, and entered the garden. When she reached for a blossom from a tree, her time came and the baby was born.

Many omens of happiness were witnessed at the time. The sun shone brighter than ever and everything in the surroundings was reflected in its golden light. The cries of wild animals were hushed, and all spiteful beings turned into lovable creatures. There were no ugly things in sight and even polluted streams became clear. The whole world was calm and peaceful.

The baby was perfect, possessing the thirty-two main features and the eighty requirements. The baby took seven steps in each direction—north, south, east, and west. With one hand pointed heavenward and the other pointed toward the earth, he said, "Above the heavens, beneath the earth, I alone am the world-honored one."

This took place five hundred and sixty-five years before Christ, or two thousand five hundred and thirteen years ago.

I am telling you the story of the birth of Buddha according to Buddhist legend. Aśvaghoṣa's *Buddhacarita,* a beautiful piece of Sanskrit literature, describes the scene vividly.

I will now introduce to you the Japanese custom for celebrating the Buddha's birthday. On the eighth of April, we Japanese Buddhists decorate the altar for the statue of the baby Buddha with many flowers and pour sweet tea over its head. The altar is called *hanami-do*, "flower pavilion," and the ceremony is called *kambutsue*, meaning "to give a bath to the baby Buddha." We think of the flower garden of Lumbinī where Buddha was born, and the sudden shower of the sweet, fragrant rain that gave the baby a natural bath. So each Buddhist temple, no matter to which sect it belongs, has an altar for the baby Buddha, covered with flowers, and the statue is placed in a bowl inside of the flower pavilion. The sweet tea, called *amacha*, is poured into this bowl. There is a ladle in the bowl, so that visitors may pour the sweet tea over the head of the baby Buddha. Some of you may be wondering what the sweet tea is. In botany, the sweet tea belongs to the genus of hydrangea. Its leaves are picked and dried well before soaking them in the hot water. It was used as a cold beverage all over Japan in olden times. Before Japanese people ever saw sugar, which came from Europe, they used this sweet tea.

The name of Buddha is quite common among Americans, and a statue of Buddha is kept in many American homes. Is it not strange to say, however, that very few Americans know who Buddha really was? And most Americans do not know what Buddhism is and what it has to do with this modern civilization of ours. Some say Buddha is a Japanese god. Some say Buddhism is an ancient teaching of India and that it has nothing to do with the current of thought in our age. They are all wrong. Buddha is neither a Japanese god nor an Indian god. We Buddhists do not worship anything. Buddhism is a teaching of enlightenment, an intellectual religion that will bring us all from delusion to realization, from suffering to peace, from the imprisonment of passions and desires to the freedom of utmost wisdom and loving-kindness. Is it not the most reliable religion of this age of free thinking and practicality?

On this birthday of Buddha, I wish to tell you what we Buddhists believe. In Christianity, no matter how faithful a believer you are, you cannot make yourself God. You cannot make yourself Christ, the anointed one. Now in Buddhism, all of you have the potential to become buddhas. Buddha is not God nor the Son of God. Buddha is a name of the condition of your mind. If you free yourself from delusions and suffering and have peace within yourself, your every action will be guided by your brilliant wisdom, and your everyday life will be nothing but the administration of your own loving-kindness. Then, are you not buddha yourself? Who said you have to suffer on account of your ancestors' sins? Don't cheat yourself! That kind of superstition is a disease of ancient ignorance. If you study Buddhism, you will know exactly and precisely who you really are. And then no myth, no legend, no superstition will mislead you.

I will tell you some anecdotes of how Zen students were enlightened, freeing themselves from all delusions.

Hyakujo, a Zen student, went out one day, attending his master, Baso. A flock of wild geese were seen flying in the sky. Baso asked, "What are they?"

"They are wild geese," answered Hyakujo.

"Where are they flying to?" asked the master.

The student answered, "They have flown away."

The master, abruptly taking hold of the student's nose, gave it a twist. Overcome with pain, the student cried out loudly, "Ouch!"

Then Baso said to him, "You say they have flown away, but all the same they have been here from the very beginning."

This made the student's back wet with cold perspiration. He was enlightened. A new buddha was born there.

Another case: Tokusan was a great scholar of the Diamond Sūtra. Learning that there was such a thing as Zen, he came to Ryūtan, the master, to be instructed in the doctrine. One day, Tokusan was sitting outside trying to look into the mystery of Zen. Ryūtan said, "Why don't you come in?"

Tokusan replied, "It is pitch dark in here."

A candle was lit and handed over to the student. When the student was at the point of taking it, the master suddenly blew out the flame, whereupon the mind of Tokusan, the student, was opened. The foundation of his delusions, namely ignorance, perished and disappeared forever.

Another case that failed: A Zen master, Echū, lived in China in olden times. One day a Zen student came and asked him about Vairocana. (Vairocana is Buddha's true body.) The master said, "Bring me some water!"

The student said, "Yes, master," and brought a pitcher of water and a cup.

The master took a drink and said, "Put away these things!"

The student said, "Yes, master," and took away the pitcher and cup.

After he returned to his seat, he asked again, "Master, I have asked you, what is Vairocana? Please tell me this time."

Then Echū said, "Oh, you are looking for that old fellow, are you not? Too bad, he passed away a long time ago."

Such a stupid Zen student! The master was showing Vairocana right in front of his nose, and he did not even glance at it. He should drink a bowlful of sweet tea. Buddha said, "If you try to see me through my form, or if you try to hear me through my voice, you cannot recognize Tathāgata. You are far away from me."

You see, Buddhism is not so easy to learn as you think. There are three steps in studying Buddhism—listening, thinking, and zazen. The above anecdotes are dealing with zazen. Those students had learned all the sūtras, had thought deeply enough to understand all the scriptures, had devoted many years to zazen, yet they could not actualize Dharma until they opened their own inner eyes.

This place was established to be the birthplace of buddha. We do not want to raise butterflies here. They fly from one teaching to another. We do not want to have the children of asuras. They fight even in the stage of babyhood. We do not want to raise monkeys and parrots here. They simply imitate what they have seen and heard. The Mentorgarten is the nursery only for baby buddhas, who love silence, and who will express loving-kindness without a word. If we do not warn each other, and watch our steps, this flower pavilion may turn into a spiritual zoo, filled with strange creatures. These creatures are born every minute, everywhere in the world. Look out!

In This Lifetime

(1949)

I could show you my clenched fist and open it—and bid you all good night.

But that is not the way things are done in the West—and so I am forced to give as a substitute, dualistic explanations, though that's not at all the way to express Zen.

Humans began by assuming that the things about which they wished to learn existed outside of themselves. Wondering what "that" is, they established "science," which is the study of *thatness*. Soon, however, they discovered that science explained only "how" things are, not "what" they are, and so humans turned inward. Seeking to understand what "this" is, they established psychology and epistemology. Together these constituted the study of *thisness*. But, paradoxically enough, when the mind itself thus became an object of study, it ceased being "this" and became "that." The experience of true thisness had been rendered impossible by the very nature of science (which can only understand thatness).

Of course Zen monks in China and Japan do not traffic at all in thisness or thatness. Somehow they manage to live quite happily and peacefully, for all that! Do you want to know the trick? They dwell in the region of what is known as *suchness*. Here is a story:

One day Seppō, a Chinese Zen master, went to the forest to cut down some trees. His disciple Chōsei accompanied him.

"Don't stop until your ax cuts the very center of the tree," said the teacher.

"I have cut it off!" answered the disciple.

Seppō said: "The old masters transmitted the teaching to their disciples from heart to heart. How is it in your own case?"

Chōsei threw his ax to the ground and said, "Transmitted!"

The teacher suddenly took his walking stick and struck his beloved disciple.

See how intimate these two woodcutters are! These monks are by nature coworkers, whether meditating in a zendo or laboring out of doors.

Some people, on the other hand, are just like actors, cooperating beautifully onstage, but once offstage, fighting together like cats in the green room. This is why Buddha prescribed that a monk's life should be as simple as possible, and used his own life as the model. The two monks in this story are true followers of Buddha. Together they carry the lamp of Dharma, the wisdom of suchness. No doubt about it!

The teacher said: "Don't stop until your ax cuts the very center of the tree." He was an expert woodsman as well as Zen master. Many Americans are currently seeking truth, visiting classes in philosophy one after another, and studying meditation under various teachers. But how many of these students are either willing or able to cut through to the tree's very core? Scratching halfheartedly around the surface of the tree, they expect someone else to cut the trunk for them. Zen wants nothing to do with such mollycoddles!

Chōsei had caught the sparkle of Zen before his teacher had even finished, and so he said, "I have cut it off!" He was such a quick worker that he thought, acted, and spoke at the same moment. *This* is realization in this lifetime.

Seppō was pleased and said: "The old masters transmitted the teaching to their disciples from heart to heart. How is it in your own case?" Chōsei threw his ax to the ground—now *that* should have been enough! I can't figure out why this upstart had to spoil everything by adding, "Transmitted!" The teacher's blow came in no time, and Chōsei certainly deserved it. We are destined to fall at the very moment we think we have attained the summit. Those who declare themselves as having attained something are not genuine Zen students. We say in Japan, "The mouth is the cause of all troubles." It sure is! When it takes in too much, it causes indigestion; when it speaks out too much, it hurts even a friend's feelings. Bashō once wrote a haiku on this; here is an English translation:

> When I say a word
> Oh my lips shiver
> In the cold wind of autumn.

Someone wrote a poem about this woodcutters' story; I will read it for you and so close my speech.

> Chōsei had a good ax.
> It was sharp enough
> To cut a stump in two
> With a single stroke.
> Seppō made his big stick
> A whetstone to sharpen it even more.

A Morning Talk

(1952)

Three Zen monks, Seppō, Kinzan, and Gantō, met one day in the temple yard. Seppō saw a water pail and pointed to it. Kinzan said, "The water is calm and the moon reflects its image." "No, no," said Seppō, "it is not water; it is not the moon." The third one, Gantō, turned over the water pail with his hands. The story ends here.

There is a gātha, which in translation might read:

The moon of the bodhisattva,
Clear and cool,
Floats in the empty sky.
If the mind of a sentient being
Tranquilizes itself
And becomes like a calm lake,
The beautiful image of Bodhi
Will appear there in no time.

Kinzan was in the same mood as this gātha when Seppō pointed to the pail; so he said, "The water is calm and the moon reflects its image." What Seppō was pointing to, however, was not the pail so much as the Buddha-body itself, which pervades the whole universe. By pointing to the pail Seppō was drawing the curtains so the entire stage could be seen and so the play could begin. Thus he said, "No, no, it is not water; it is not the moon." What Seppō had in mind was noumenon, not phenomenon. Although Seppō improved upon Kinzan's response, Gantō wiped away all traces by turning over the water pail; his action vividly reveals the nature of true emancipation.

In the Vedanta one finds a pantheistic doctrine according to which Brahman is the ultimate reality, and all phenomena are real only in virtue of their relation to and unification with Brahman. From this point of view, nothing real exists outside Brahman. As it is expressed in the Upanisads: "There is One only, without Second." Seppō's view is similar to this Vedanta doctrine. Gantō's action goes beyond this kind of Vedanta monism by showing that ultimate reality admits of secondness as well; it is One in a sense which is not the opposite of Second, but is beyond the distinction between oneness and secondness. It has been said (I believe by Professor Takakusu) that in Buddhism a man does not join himself to Buddha to become one. He merely frees himself from his delusions and becomes buddha. If a thousand persons attain realization, there are one thousand buddhas.

This statement clarifies the Buddhist understanding of oneness. D.T. Suzuki has said:

> To define exactly the Buddhistic notion of the highest being, it may be convenient to borrow the term coined by a German scholar, "panentheism," according to which God is all and one and more than the totality of existence.

From a sermon of his teacher, Sōyen Shaku, he quotes the following:

> Religion is not to go to God by forsaking the world, but to find Him in it. Our faith is to believe in our essential oneness with Him and not in our sensuous separateness. "God is in us and we in Him," must be made the most fundamental faith of all religions.[18]

In this morning's story, when Kinzan says, "The water is calm and the moon reflects its image," one is reminded of the Gospel of John: "All mine are thine and thine are mine; and I am glorified in them." These words carry with them a slight echo of separateness, so Seppō insists, "No, no, it is not water; it is not the moon." For him, there is only One, without Second. But Gantō, having no patience with any form of conceptualization, over-turns the pail to expose the thing itself! Such action is Zen in practical life.

Zen is not a sect or religion; nor is it a school of philosophy. It is not enough to tell people that it is possible to become a buddha. What Zen does is actually to produce buddhas! One thousand realizations, one thousand buddhas. I once asked Suzuki, "What is panentheism?" And he told me he had never used such a word—at least not as far as Zen is concerned. He thereby played the same trick Gantō did.

Genrō wrote a poem about this story:

> In the garden of willows and flowers,
> On the tower of beautiful music,

Two guests are enjoying wine,
Holding their golden cups
Under the pale light of the moon.
A nightingale starts suddenly
From the branch of a tree,
Dew dropping from the twigs.

Fūgai, Genrō's disciple, comments: "Nightingale? No. It is a phoenix!"

On Nirvāṇa Day (I)

(February 15, 1952)

Buddha Sākyamuni passed from the world in the grove of Sala trees, not far from the river Hiranyavati, near the capital of Kushinara, in the north-eastern part of India. It was four hundred and eighty-five years before the Christian era, 2,437 years ago. We Buddhists call the death of Buddha *Parinirvāṇa,* meaning, "to enter the region beyond birth and death."

On Monday and Friday evenings, at seven o'clock, we have zazen, and those who are interested are welcome to attend, regardless of nationality, religion, sex, or age. There is no membership obligation. Those who are satisfied with my way as host, may come and spend an evening in this zendo. Equanimity is the way of living for a Buddhist monk. Therefore, you may be unable to get an impression of entertainment, but I know you will feel the spirit of peacefulness in the calm atmosphere.

Buddhism is a philosophy that requires one to study many years, but at the same time it is merely a way of living that will lead anyone into the pure and unselfish life. Buddha preached for forty-nine years and solved all problems of life with his enlightened mind. There are many teachings in Buddhism higher than the most profound philosophy of modern times, and the more you study them, the more you will be convinced of the penetrating wisdom of Buddha, who lived some twenty-four centuries ahead of us.

The teaching is meant to be practiced in our everyday lives. Buddhism is the simplest and easiest philosophy, as it is based on pure reasoning of human experience, and has nothing to do with legends and traditions of a particular nation.

When the Buddha was about to pass from this world, some of his disciples were attending him in grave silence. Under the moonlight, at the hour of midnight, he summarized his teaching for them. He said, "After I have gone, you must respect and practice *pratimokṣa,* that is, the set of ethical precepts I have prescribed for you. Let it be to you as a light in the darkness and as a treasure to a poor man. Let it be your great teacher hereafter. Even if I dwelt longer in this world, I would repeat the same things. You who live in my teaching should keep yourselves pure, should take care of your health, and should have your meals regularly. You are working for your spiritual emancipation, therefore you must keep your minds quiet, in the right attitude. Do not hide your own faults. Do not show people any strange actions but conduct yourselves in a becoming manner. Should the people help you with clothes, food, shelter, or medicine, you may accept them in the name of the highest wisdom, but always be satisfied with bare necessities. The foregoing words deal with the last general application of my teaching."

And at last, the Buddha said, "Behold now, brother monks, I exhort you, saying—Decay is inherent in all component things. Work out your own emancipation with diligence!"

What do you think of these last words of Buddha? He did not say he was an agent of a supreme being. He did not say he could blot out the stain of sins. He said only, "Work out your own emancipation with diligence!"

Who cannot accept such a plain and independent statement? Is there God above us? Is there no God outside of the universe? Buddhism does not bother with such foolish questions. Is there the creator of the world or not? Is there the ruler of the universe or not? Buddhism ignores such useless questions.

Buddha said in the Dhammapāda, "All that we are is the result of what we have thought; it is founded on our thoughts; it is made up of our thoughts. If a man speaks or acts with an evil thought, pain follows him, as the wheel follows the foot of him who draws the carriage. All that we are is the result of what we have thought; it is founded on our thoughts; it is made up of our thoughts. If a man speaks or acts with a pure thought, happiness follows him like a shadow that never leaves him."

What do you think of these words of Buddha? There is no way to be saved unless you save yourselves. Buddhism or no Buddhism, this is a self-evident fact.

When I take a walk along Broadway, I always admire the well disciplined manners of the American public. Hundreds and hundreds of people come and go, making a lively stream of human interest. The huge crowd moves on gracefully. There is no pushing, no jostling against one another. They simply walk along easily and freely, as if they were in their own private rooms. Each individual, however, carries his or her own problem and strives or struggles along with his or her task. There is ambition and here is adventure. There is pathos in love affairs and here is disappointment in business. In fact, a teardrop expresses tragedy and the sound of laughter echoes profound philosophy. So, after all, they are not mere peaceful pedestrians. They are a mass of tumult, entangled with thousands and thousands of circumstances. In the Buddhist view, they are playing together a tragicomedy of karma on the most uncertain stage which they themselves call a world. I do not know whether we should congratulate each other or not. But one thing is sure. Each of us is a member of this great theatrical company and each of us is playing our own selected role, every day, every hour, and every minute.

The word *karma* is a Sanskrit noun in the nominative case and is derived from the verb *kar* which means "to do." In the objective case, it is *karma,* and the Pali words *kamma* and *kamman* correspond to the Sanskrit. The word *karma* is almost anglicized now, and is treated as an English word in many dictionaries.

The karma process was in early times the doctrine of the Brahmans and Buddhists, and it has remained a typical feature in the faith and philosophical thought of India. All states and conditions in this life are the direct consequences of actions done in a previous existence. Every deed or action done in the present life determines the future. Therefore, human life is nothing but the working process of karma—the endless series of cause and effect.

Life is a sort of dance. The children of the world are playing their game—all kinds of games. They form a group and dance around their own maypoles. When I lived in San Francisco I used to watch the happy dancing of children around the maypole every May Day. It was my optimistic viewpoint of the karmic world.

I see, however, the people of the world clinging fatally to their maypoles. When they fall, they dumbfoundedly lose their entire interest in life. They want to stay as children the rest of their lives. Such people are clinging to the delusion of individual soul, the existence of which Buddhism denies strongly. They do not want to think. They should act as grown men and women and dance around the world freely, without fastening themselves to the maypole.

The karma theory of Buddhism gives you the idea of the immortality of work, instead of the immortality of soul. Your soul does not exist as an ego-entity; but it will continue in the work that you do, in the sentiments that you feel, and in the thoughts that you think. And thus, you will live forever in these. When we stand before a canvas painted by a great painter, we feel the presence of the artist; his ideas and feelings are embodied in it. We say that the artist is still living in the work. We do not know if his soul has gone up to heaven and is enjoying celestial happiness, but we do know that he is certainly still living among ourselves, and is inspiring us to the higher ideals of life.

Our existence is a sort of link in the eternal chain of cause and effect. We have not come on earth to assert only our individuality. Our karma is most solidly linked to our ancestors and their civilization, as well as to our successors and their destiny.

If we fail to enrich and ennoble our spiritual inheritance, which originally came from the Mind Essence, we entirely ignore the meaning of the history of humanity, we altogether disregard our responsibility to our forefathers and grandchildren. Therefore we must behave nobly, we must think rationally, and we must feel unselfishly. Thus, we live in the karma which endures forever, even after the dissolution of this physical existence.

According to Buddhism, this universe is a sort of spiritual laboratory, in which all our ideal possibilities are experimented upon, developed, and perfected. When this material garment wears out after long use, we throw it away, put on a new one, and appear in the same laboratory as our own successors.

Let me remind you: we do not go anywhere else, not even to Heaven. Let us remain in this universe. Let the karma we have accumulated here bear its fruit and be brought to a happy consummation. This is the teaching of Buddha Sākyamuni.

With a Pali formula, praising the highest wisdom, I close my speech.

Namo tasso bhagavato arahato samma sambuddhassa!

On Nirvāṇa Day (II)

(February 15, 1953)

Bodhisattvas: This morning I am going to show you my translations of two Chinese poems. They are Zen poems commemorating Buddha's Parinirvāṇa. This first was written in China during the Sung Dynasty:

The wind shakes the thready willow to show the devil's dance.
The soft rain sprinkles over the flowers to wash the tears
    of Ānanda.
The golden-faced Gautama! Where did he go?
Thousands and thousands of followers are disheartened
    in the scene.

Buddha passed away in the year 485 B.C., or 2,438 years ago. The Chinese believe the date to be the fifteenth of February of the lunar calendar.

The monk-poet who wrote this poem, even though he lived in China seventeen centuries after Buddha, described the nirvāṇa scene vividly. The first line: "The wind shakes the thready willow to show the devil's dance," makes me believe that the monk-poet must have seen, beyond time and distance, the actual place in India where the devils danced just after the death of Buddha.

In the second line he wrote: "The soft rain sprinkles over the flowers to wash the tears of Ānanda."

You all know how Ānanda, the beloved disciple of Buddha, grieved to part from his teacher. The poet saw the spring flowers of China as the gentle face of Ānanda. The third line asks an important question. "The golden-faced Gautama! Where did he go?" Yes, indeed, where did he go? This is the kōan for us this very morning. Bodhisattvas, are you going to waste these spring days without knowing where the Buddha went? This is not history study class. Show me your Zen this instant!

The monk's last line: "Thousands and thousands of followers are disheartened in the scene." Not only the direct disciples who were left by Buddha in the olden times, but all followers of the golden-faced Gautama, throughout the world, are disheartened, even today.

The next selection is from the works of Daichi, a Sōtō master of Japan who lived in the fourteenth century.

Dark shadows of the willow trees!
White flowers of the early spring!
On a day in the second month of the lunar calendar,
In the Sala forest, Buddha entered into Parinirvāṇa.
The disciples wrapped his remains around and around with pale,
    white cloth.
Yet the brilliance of this golden body penetrates through all
    covers and illuminates the surroundings.

In the sūtras, the burial of Buddha is described in detail. Our poem depicts the facts and also beautifies the devotion of the disciples to their teacher.

We disciples had to bow when we passed by the bedroom of our teacher, Sōyen Shaku, even though the door was shut and we knew that he was sleeping. With such experience, I appreciate this poem very much.

Buddhism is an exiled religion. The people of India did not keep it long. The believers of opposite teachings destroyed temples, pagodas, and statues. They buried what they could not destroy. Dharma, however, will spread in other lands like the brilliance of Buddha's body, which effuses forth through all covers.

Buddhism in Japan is suffering these days from self-poisoning. The splendor of the temples is covering the true spirit of the pāramitās. Priest-craft is corroding bodhisattvahood and no one cares about *śīla* and *dhyāna* anymore. Dharma, however, is crossing the Pacific Ocean, and permeating the American mind.

Dharmakāya

(undated)

In eighteenth-century Japan there lived a Buddhist scholar by the name of Tōrei. Although he had studied all existing sūtras, he had been unable to attain enlightenment, because his mind persisted in aimless wandering about the universe, still the victim of dualistic ideas. Even a great scholar like Tōrei continued to cling to the world of desire, of form and of no-form. While on a theoretical level he firmly believed that these aspects of the universe were nothing but *Mu,* on a practical level he was unable to enter deeply enough into meditation, and so could not attune himself with Dharmakāya—that is, unite himself with the universe in its actual nothingness.

One day—all of a sudden—he cast off his clinging ideas and entered at last into the region of absoluteness. His mind became like a naked body, and for him Nirvāṇa was "visible and present, inviting all to come and see," just as the Buddha had said. He was enlightened; he attained realization. Like the smashing of a glass basin or the demolishing of a house of jade, he was awakened and entered into the palace of nothingness. He found buddha within him; he saw his original nature face to face; he heard the sound of one hand. Looking up at the sky and laughing loudly, he exclaimed: "Oh how great is Dharmakāya! How great and immense that which exists forevermore!" He wrote a Chinese poem, which translated into English would be:

Dharmakāya, Dharmakāya!
I see you as a mountain leaning on the sky.
I see you as a rapid, constantly running cascade.
The teaching of Buddha is my own now.
I am the master of this flowery spring.

When Buddha was alive in this world, some of his disciples—those enthusiastic in meditation—acquired realization without difficulty. Others, chanting *"Buddham saranam gacchami,"* worshipped Buddha as someone superhuman. These disciples neglected their own buddhahood, which lies within the hearts of all, awaiting only our cultivation of it. For these disciples, Buddha's words and actions were merely external paradigms. Chanting *"Dhammam saranam gacchami,"* they became homeless monks, establishing the Buddhist Order in accordance with the laws and regulations Buddha had formulated. Having found a harmonious life in this way, they chanted *"Sangham saranam gacchami."*[19]

After Buddha passed away, those monks who had forgotten their own inner treasure erected images of him and worshipped them as their teacher, chanting *"Buddham saranam gacchami."* Though beautiful of heart, these monks were blind to the higher wisdom; chanting *"Dhammam saranam gacchami,"* they clung to the words of the Buddha, worshipping the sūtras instead of their own Buddha-nature. Thinking that as long as they stayed within the Order they were leading a pure and happy life, they chanted *"Sangham saranam gacchami."*

Even today, such monks can be found. They are keeping the Three Treasures, but theirs are merely historical treasures. They fail to realize that there is a real Buddha—Dharmakāya, the substance of the universe; that there are many millions of unwritten sūtras in this world, manifesting the truth of this universe; and that there are many ideal stages of life that emerge in the course of human struggle. Although these monks call themselves Buddhists, in my eyes they are completely petrified, with no spirit, no life, no active power within them.

Bodhisattvas, you have chosen to be Zen Buddhists—that is, rational and practical Buddhists. Though you chant in the name of the Three Treasures just as those lifeless monks do, your Buddha is not an object of hero-worship; your Dharma is not reducible to written sūtras; and your Sangha is more than merely a group of monks and nuns. Buddha said: "If you try to see me through my form, if you try to hear me through my voice, you will never reach me. Such a person is a stranger to my teaching."

When you, as bodhisattvas, chant *"Buddham saranam gacchami,"* you should try to attune yourself with the universe, until you are able to see its substance as your own. When you chant *"Dhammam saranam gacchami,"* try to perceive the unwritten laws of the universe. And when you chant *"Sangham saranam gacchami,"* try to realize that your everyday life is nothing but your emancipated mind in action. Remember always that you are bodhisattvas, and as bodhisattvas stand three thousand feet taller than those petrified monks and nuns!

At the door of our zendo in San Francisco hung a verse from a Chinese poem, the translation of which is:

> Who said Buddha passed away from us?
> If you enter into deep meditation,
> You will see him every day.

Once I saw a mounted scroll written by Tesshu Yamaoka, a well-known Zen student who, though only an upāsaka or layman, almost reached the stage of Zen master. The English translation would be:

> Falling blossoms lie scattered on the ground.
> No one tries to sweep them up.
> Birds are singing the melody of spring.
> Undisturbed, the guest is at rest in his land of dreams.

Isn't this the picture of true calmness itself? Nirvāṇa beckons from this verse. Of what use are millions of gold pieces in this land of calmness? What can you do with the trash of book-learning in this fairyland of everlastingness? Your fame, your beauty, all your so-called power and strength—these are merely the toys of a nightmare of the past. Unless you enter once into this world of nothingness, you will miss something. The gate of the palace of realization may be entered while sipping tea. Yes, in a cup of tea you may be fortunate enough to find Zen. Let's have some tea!

Commemoration of Buddha's Realization

(December 6, 1953)

We are celebrating Buddha's enlightenment today. The date should be December 8, but for the convenience of both Japanese and American friends, I have set this day for the gathering.

In China, the Zen students say, "Bodhidharma never came to China and the Second Patriarch, Eka, never went to India." So we should consider that Buddha was never enlightened in India and that Bodh Gaya, the place where he was enlightened, does not belong to any particular country.

Buddhists in Ceylon, Burma, and Thailand think of Bodh Gaya as the most important place in the history of Buddhism and have tried for the past hundred years to buy it back from the owners, a Brahmin family who believe in teachings other than Buddhism. These Buddhists tried every method but were unable to succeed, as the place is an historical site which draws pilgrims from all over the world and is, thus, income producing.

Time is, however, the best cure for all troubles, for this year the Indian Republic made arrangements to return the holy place unconditionally to the Buddhists of the world. It is very pleasant news to hear this. But I am afraid that in the future, those who cling to formality will make it a mecca for Buddhists. They will draw more throngs from all over the world, thus showing the ugliness of attachment and priestcraft, over and over again.

I have with me my teacher Sōyen Shaku's diary from which I will read in English translation of his visit to Bodh Gaya, dated August 1, 1906.

The weather was very uncertain and at 3:25 A.M. I reached the station by buggy where I awaited the arrival of the train that belongs to the Gaya Branch. The train came and we started at 5:10 A.M., reaching Gaya Station at 10:05 in the morning.

Hiring a buggy, I hurried to Bodh Gaya, though the driver was so unkind to the little horse that I finally gave him some money and asked him to be more compassionate.

We could see the river Nairanyana on the left side, and on the right, the Sala trees grew here and there, looking as if they were using the space as a pasture.

At twelve o'clock, we reached Bodh Gaya.

I had understood that there was a Japanese man who stayed there, paying homage to the holy place, and I had planned to look him up. His name was Tokumyō Fujita. I asked the guide about him and he told me that Mr. Fujita had passed away only a few days before, on July 27. I therefore paid a visit to his grave, and many thoughts of Buddhism came and went in my mind, since having to arise early, I had not slept well. I had been traveling alone, and now, the one Japanese with whom I thought that I could meet and talk to, heart to heart, was gone. This made me very sad even though I had never met him. The guide told me that Mr. Fujita had firm faith in Buddhism and that he had come to India several years before and had stayed at this place as though he were serving a living buddha.

I found a member of the Mahābodhi Society of Ceylon, the Venerable M. Sumangala, with whom I talked in my half-forgotten Sinhalese. This monk stays here all the time to do services for the pilgrims. He led me to the seat under the Bodhi tree to pay homage there to Buddha, who, more than two thousand years ago, attained enlightenment under the burning sun.

I had heard about this place and had thought of visiting it for over thirty years, but was unable to fulfill my wish until this day. Twenty years ago, I had gone to Ceylon and remained there for three years, but could not find the opportunity then to journey here. Now I had come after a long trip through Europe, on my way home to Japan. Tears of gladness fell from my eyes. I could not help it. I took out my brush and ink and wrote a poem:

> Came to the holy place afar,
> Gladness and sadness stir my heart,
> The ancient seat of Buddha!
> I feel his presence even now.
> The cool shadow of the Bodhi tree
> Gradually calms my mind.
> Birds of the forest sing the tune of samscritam.
> Atmosphere of Gaya speaks of asamscritam.
> I raise my head to see the face of Tathāgatha,
> I only see the evening sun hanging above the blue
> > mountains.

After reciting this poem, I paid homage at the Buddha temple, the stupa, and other places, and then returned to my lodging. There I talked with the monk, Sumangala, in my incomplete English and Sinhalese. He told me that the place is owned by a Brahmin priest named Mahan. He is very wealthy and powerful. Years ago, Dhammapāla of Ceylon made every effort to buy Bodh Gaya from him, but was refused. The place now is a sort of village of beggars who beg alms from pilgrims and workers who, with their families, labor hard on the estate.

At 3 P.M., during a thunderstorm, I hired a buggy and drove about seven miles until I reached the town of Gaya itself.

This is the conclusion of my teacher's account of his visit to Bodh Gaya. Buddha attained his enlightenment at the age of thirty-five, in 530 B.C., 2,483 years ago.

My gātha today is an epilogue to this diary passage.

> We have cultivated the Buddha-field in this pure Zen
> > atmosphere.
> Everyone is encouraged by the ancient anecdote of Gaya.

Even the late rice crops must be harvested this time.

Lamp of Dharma burns eternally while the winter rain patters on our window.

Have a Cup of Tea[20]

(undated)

One time long ago in China there was a white-haired priest famous for his greeting. As students would arrive for zazen he would say to them, "Have a cup of tea." When an old monk would come to his room, the greeting would be the same. Often strangers would stroll by the temple gate, and after asking them to come in and seating them on tatami near the Buddha, he would have a cup of tea with them. Eventually his young assistant grew weary of the repetition of "Have a cup of tea" night and day, and so said to the priest: "Why do you have to keep repeating the same thing over and over again?" Looking into the young man's eyes, the old priest replied: "Have a cup of tea."

Zen monks are unique people—fanciful and bizarre, spontaneous action comes naturally to them. They are full of whimsy and surprise. Though conventional people consider them eccentric and strange, they sail on through, oblivious to the world's opinions and judgments, like ships keeping an even keel on high seas. I am one of these strange monks; I too like to say, "Have a cup of tea."

Once you have lifted your cup, turn it twice and bow. Something happens in the taking of tea that is more than tea and more than politeness. Two can turn to one and the taste be filled with wonder.

One day at dusk an American tourist dropped some coins into a box at the entrance to a Japanese Buddhist shrine. After pulling the cord, to which a bell was attached, she bowed before the Buddha. A priest came out from the shadows and, bowing in turn, beckoned to her. As she went toward him he said, "This is the first time I have ever seen a tourist bow. Won't you come in and have a cup of tea?" They sat together on a tatami behind the huge bronze Buddha. He lit some incense and a candle, and, placing them on a low table close by, began to talk. He had been to America ten years before. He wondered how life was there now. With television and highways, all of that speed and power, he wondered what effect such things were having on the individual citizen. Speaking with affection of Whitman, Thoreau, and James, remarking how Zen they were,

Nyogen Senzaki in Kyoto, Japan. November 3, 1955

he said: "American youth will learn from them." Then in silence he whisked the tea—young leaves from old trees grown in the shade, old leaves from young trees grown in the sun. The sun had gone down; dark shadows moved across the paper door. As his guest prepared to leave, he placed a bundle in the palm of her hand. Prayer beads. His own. "These beads are old. I am old. Please take them to America and keep them near you." She looked up at him and bowed.

Yes, it is the taste that matters—the flavor of the moment, of people and places. When I make a cup of tea for a guest, I become a servant; when my guest receives the cup with naturalness and ease, he becomes the host. This is the taste of tea and the essence of ceremony.

Most Zen monks are indifferent to formal skills, styles, and techniques. They prefer to improvise, in accordance with place, mood, and people. Once a friend of mine—a monk from another temple—took five Zen students to the country, where they walked in the woods, rode bicycles, swam, and danced in the moonlight. When the air became chilly and darkness descended, they lit lanterns and retired to a rustic shelter. In a cluster of pines, facing a walled-in garden, they picnicked around a low wooden table next to a burning stove. When the water began to boil it sounded like a soft breeze coming through a pine forest. The night was shadowy and still.

My friend the priest turned to his hostess and asked her to bring him the largest bowl she had. She went to the kitchen and returned with a vegetable dish made of clay in the shape of a giant cup. Sitting at the head of the table, my friend looked out into the night, smiled a quiet smile to the guests—most of whom had been trained in ceremonial tea; one was even a teacher from Tōkyō—and bowed. "I will now present a most presumptuous bowl of tea," he said. With precise gestures and a gentle elegance he folded paper napkins and placed one in front of each person. The student next to him picked up her sandwich, breaking the bread into small pieces, which she passed around the table. With a simple but courtly grace the priest picked up a tin spoon and scooped out seven portions of powdered green tea. Then he poured boiling water into the bowl, and whisked it until a jade-green froth appeared on the surface. He turned the bowl twice, putting the most beautiful side away from himself and toward his guests—some of whom were old, some young, some Eastern, some Western, some Jewish, some Buddhist, and some Christian. Each in his turn took the bread and ate. Each one drank from the same cup. Then the priest began to chant, the soft tones of his voice flowing through the very bloodstreams of the assembled guests. At that moment, everybody was nobody. Like the table. Like the bowl and sky. A sip of Zen. A sip of tea. Or was it wine and a wafer?

[from a eulogy by one of Senzaki's students:] Nyogen Senzaki began this tale of greeting—but now he is alone. "Like a mushroom in a nameless mountain."[21] *Without wine. Without bread. Without tea, or even a sweet. But to us he keeps saying, "Have a cup of tea"—with a taste of Zen!*

Nyogen Senzaki's Prayer

(undated)

Dharmakāya is the Buddha's holy body. It is the everlasting sea of the eternal reality of the universe. From this transcendental point of view, there is no coming of Buddha, and so there is no going of Buddha. Yet in the endless sea of phenomena arise waves of charity and loving-kindness to enlighten the ignorance of all fellow beings. The eternal reality reveals its loving-kindness in the manifestation of the waves of phenomena. Thus, from the phenomenal point of view, there is the coming of Buddha, and so there is the going of Buddha.

My first prayer is that I might make myself a mirror of Dharmakāya, reflecting the whole world and all beings therein.

My last prayer is that the everlasting waves will carry us all to emancipation, that we may enter the flowery garden of buddhahood. My adoration is for the knowledge of all buddhas; and I shall devote my life to the enlightenment of myself and others.

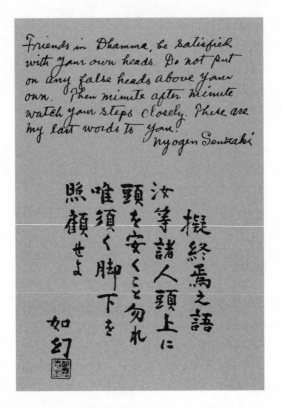

My Last Words

(June 16, 1957)

It pleases me very much to meet you in this sanctuary, to meditate together and to recite the Four Vows in Japanese. Your kind thoughts and noble deeds have encouraged me to prolong my life more than I expected. I feel very grateful to you all.

Once I imagined that I was going away from this world, leaving all of you behind, and I thus wrote my last words in English.

Friends in Dhamma, be satisfied with your own heads. Do not put on any false heads above your own. Then minute after minute, watch your steps closely. These are my last words to you.

What do you think of these words? I think I owe you some explanation. Each head of each one of you is the noblest thing in the whole universe. No God, no buddha, no sage, no master can reign over it.

Rinzai said: "If you master your own situation, wherever you stand is the land of truth." How many of our fellow beings can prove the truthfulness of Rinzai's words by action?

Henri Bergson says:

The spectacle of what religions have been in the past, of what certain religions still are today, is indeed humiliating for human intelligence. What a farrago of error and folly! Experience may indeed say "that is false" and reasoning "that is absurd." Humanity only clings all the more to that absurdity and that error.... Homo sapiens, the only creature endowed with reason, is also the only creature to pin its existence to things unreasonable.

You see, this Frenchman is quite indignant toward those who put false heads above their own.

Fellow students, you are the only group in the western lands to show this French philosopher how to shut his mouth. But, to do so, you must try to live in Zen. To live in Zen, you must watch your steps minute after minute, closely. As I have always told you, you should be mindful of your feet, not of your head or chest, in your meditation as well as in your everyday life. Keep your head cool but your feet warm! Do not let your sentiments sweep you off your feet!

Well-trained Zen students should breathe with their feet, not with their lungs. This means that you should forget your lungs and only be conscious of your feet while breathing. The head is the sacred part of your body. Let it do its own work, but do not make any "monkey business" with it.

These days I have been speaking about "awareness of breath," but to do it practically, you should try to pull down your inhalation to the bottom of your feet and then from there bring up your exhalation slowly—I am not speaking physiologically, but only about your attitude. Such striving is realization itself.

As Buddha himself was cremated, my corpse should be treated in the same way.

The funeral must be performed in the simplest way. A few friends who live nearby may attend it quietly. Those who know how to recite sūtras may murmur the shortest one. That will be enough. Do not ask a priest or anyone to make a long service and speech and have others yawn. Silence is the best offering to me!

Send out the only announcement of my death to Sōen Nakagawa, Ryūtaku Monastery, Japan. Other friends will find out the news sooner or later. Why should we disturb them in a hurry!

Everything in this meditation hall belongs to the Saṅgha—there is nothing to be called mine. If Sōen-san takes charge of this zendo, he will take care of everything.

My passport should be returned to the Japanese authorities, and the report of my death should be made lawfully. I am a man without a country but, after all, the law is the law. I am a homeless monk, therefore there is nothing to be left to anyone. Until Sōen-san comes to America, Shūbin and Hakkan will take care of all things I left behind.

Sōen-san will take care of my Japanese manuscripts. It is not necessary to publish them, but have others read them freely when they wish to do so. I wish Sōen-san to take care of the English manuscripts too, consulting with Kangetsu and Shōhō in the same manner as with the Japanese ones.

Remember me as a monk, and nothing else. I do not belong to any sect or cathedral. None of them should send me a promoted priest's rank or anything of that sort. I wish to be free from such trash and die happily.

However innumerable all beings are, I vow to save them all;
However inexhaustible our delusions are, I vow to extinguish them all;

However immeasurable the Dharma Teachings are, I vow to master
  them all;
However endless the Buddha's Way is, I vow to follow it.
                                                —The Four Bodhisattva Vows

Remarks Made at the Funeral of Nyogen Senzaki

(May 12, 1958)

"Bodhisattvas"— "fellow students"—How often have we heard Nyogen
Senzaki address us in these terms when we gathered with him in his
zendo?

"Bodhisattvas," because Sensei realized the possibilities, indeed
believed in the ultimate certainty, that all of us would some time attain
realization and in turn endeavor to help others.

"Fellow students," because Senzaki-san never considered himself in
any superior position. "I have never made any demarcation of my learning," he recently wrote, "and do not consider myself finished at any
point." If called "Master" he laughed, claiming to be nothing more than
a homeless monk after the tradition of the first Saṅgha. He welcomed
us, subtly guiding us, as fellow students seeking realization—even while
telling us there was nothing to seek. The English name he chose for his
zendo (Mentorgarten), whether located on Turner Street, in a hotel
room, on East Second, or in San Francisco, implies a garden where people gather in the pursuit of wisdom—prajñā, if you like. "No one, no
thing, can be more than a finger pointing," he often said, adding that
the pointer should never be taken for that which was indicated.

His first school, after leaving his teacher, the Rōshi Sōyen Shaku, was
for children, in Aomori Prefecture, Japan. He always loved children, and
perhaps in changing the word kindergarten to Mentorgarten he realized
that we are all children in a sense, whatever our ages; children wishing to

mature in a larger sense than that normally prescribed by the life span. Certainly the complexities and artificialities of sophisticated adult living were not for him—though this was in no sense a shirking of adult responsibilities.

Undoubtedly the life of the monastery would have been more attractive than the course he chose. He might have achieved fame as a master had he remained at Engaku Temple, in Kamakura. But his way was to be of service in the world, whether to children and nursemaids at an army post, to fellow Japanese, or to those of another race in a far-off, foreign land. When he came to America more than half a century ago his chief regret was that another monk, whom he considered more qualified, had been killed in the Russo-Japanese war and therefore could not make the journey. When his teacher, Sōyen Shaku, suggested that he stay, such was his respect, his nature, and his resolution that he remained in America for more than fifty years before returning to his native country for a visit.

Nor was he subsidized in any way to carry on the work of Zen in this country. Completely dependent on his own efforts for food and lodging, he worked at such jobs as he could find: houseboy, apprentice cook—no job was too menial, or to be considered as other than in the natural course of events. He saved his money, living very frugally, not to hoard it, nor to satisfy longings for comfort or pleasure, but so that he might rent a hall and discuss Zen Buddhism, where others might join him in meditation and study. He called the various meeting places a "Floating Zendo" until 1928, when a regular place was acquired in San Francisco. "When I came to Los Angeles in 1931," he said recently, "I carried the zendo with me as a silkworm carries a cocoon. The silk thread surrounds me unbroken. It may weave a brocade of autumn leaves or a spotless spring kimono for the coming year. I only feel gratitude to my teachers and all my friends, and fold my hands, palm to palm."

No one can doubt that Senzaki-san could have built a temple and organized a numerous following, particularly since the war, as Zen has gained the attention of scholars, writers, and artists in the Western world until it is today almost a cult in certain circles. Sensei certainly could have attracted wider attention and fame. But name and fame, money and position, gain and loss were never alluring to him, nor did they seem substantial to a true Zen influence. And, of course, he recognized in them the seeds of distraction, ambition, and suffering so responsible for many of today's ills. His was the solitary path which each must ultimately take for himself. Thus he avoided anything that smacked of proselytizing; he offered no inducements, no mysteries or attendant rites which so easily become substitutes for the realization of oneself by himself, and for the compassion which must possess each heart.

His way was ever the humble—but we know him without any eulogy. To use the Zen phrase he loved, these words but paint legs on a snake. They cannot add to his worth, they cannot honor him sufficiently, and they cannot adequately express our sense of loss. Senzaki-san needs no justification; he wanted no eulogy. We can honor him best with renewed efforts to realize our own essential nature and by making more room in our hearts for compassion for our fellow beings. As for our own sorrow, let us remember what Sensei said about the flow of life, and that as each birth is a death, each death is a birth.

For some of us the silence surrounding the form, and the intervals between the syllables of a brief haiku, express more than all the words that have been said:

> The chill of winter this May night—
> A fallen leaf
> In the spring garden.
>
> —Shōhō

Glossary

ĀLAYA (ĀLAYAVIJÑĀNA) In Buddhist philosophy, ālaya (*araya, arayashiki,* J.) is the eighth of the eight consciousnesses and is often referred to as the repository or store consciousness, because in it all experiences are contained and recorded. See D.T. Suzuki's *Studies in the Lankāvatāra Sūtra.*

ANUTTARA-SAMYAK-SAMBODHI Perfect or supreme enlightenment; the unsurpassed wisdom of the buddhas.

ASURA A demon who fights against devas (gods); in Buddhism, a demon of a warlike nature. Asuras are said to be one world below human beings in the sixfold classification of the transmigrational worlds.

ATMAN The individual self, soul, or ego, as contrasted to the supreme or universal self. Essential to Buddhism, as opposed to Hinduism, is the rejection of the atman.

AVATAMSAKA SŪTRA The Mahāyāna scripture that is the source of the Hua-yen or Kegon school of Buddhism, which teaches the doctrine of totality or interpenetration. See D.T. Suzuki's Third Series of *Essays in Zen Buddhism* for a commentary and partial translation.

BAHA'ISM A religious sect founded in Iran in the nineteenth century that believes in the spiritual unity of humankind, world peace, universal education, and the equality of men and women.

BASHŌ MATSUO (1644–94) The great Japanese haiku poet, Zen student, and traveler, whose life and poetry were direct expressions of Zen.

BASO DŌITSU (?–788) One of the great Chinese Zen masters (Mazu, Ch.) of the Tang Dynasty. A disciple of Nangaku Ejō (Nanyue Huairang, Ch.). It is said that Baso had over three hundred Dharma heirs. See Nyogen Senzaki's *Ripe, Unripe Fruit,* p. 136 in this volume.

BHIKṢUS, BHIKṢUṆĪS Monks and nuns, respectively.

BODHI Perfect wisdom or enlightenment. Its meaning has been well expressed in this famous verse by Huineng, the Sixth Patriarch of Zen in China:

> The mind is the Bodhi tree of perfect wisdom;
> The body is the stand of a bright mirror.
> The bright mirror is originally clear and pure.
> Where has it been defiled by any dust?

BODHICITTA Literally "Buddha Mind." (See Zen.)

BODHIDHARMA The Indian master who arrived in China in 520 and became the First Patriarch of Zen in China. The question "Why did Bodhidharma come from India to China?" is an important kōan in Zen practice. Bodhidharma, a master of Buddha-Hridaya (Buddha's Mind), brought with him not books but the practice of zazen. Although not much is known of his life, it seems he was of royal birth, and is reputed to have remained in zazen-seclusion for nine years after his well-known encounter with the Chinese Emperor Wu. His most famous successor was the Chinese priest Daiso Eka (Dazu Huike, Ch.). Bodhidharma died either in 528 or 536, and was given the posthumous title of *Engaku Daishi*, which means "Great Teacher of Complete Enlightenment."

BODHISATTVA *Bosatsu* or *bōsa* in Japanese; literally, *bodhi* means "enlightened" and *sattva* means "being." A bodhisattva is one who realizes that all beings—not just human beings, even a speck of dust—are primarily buddhas (enlightened ones), and seeks to share the joy of this realization with others, so they themselves may experience this truth. Although it is commonly said that bodhisattvas postpone their own emancipation until all sentient beings have been saved, the plain fact is that bodhisattvas cannot help others unless they are themselves enlightened; the real driving power behind their work derives from their own realization. Nonetheless, it is true that, unlike the śrāvaka or pratyekabuddha, the bodhisattva is not concerned with his or her own enlightenment as an end in itself, but as a way of bringing about universal liberation from delusion and suffering. The bodhisattva ideal is the heart of Mahāyāna Buddhism.

BOSATSU See Bodhisattva.

BRAHMA One of the Hindu trinity, along with Vishnu and Shiva.

BRAHMAN Ultimate Reality according to the Vedanta philosophy.

BUDDHA Literally "enlightened one." There are many different points of view from which one can speak of "Buddha." Historically the term refers to Siddhartha Gautama, or Śākyamuni Buddha (563–483 B.C.), the actual founder of Buddhism in India. But in an extended sense, Śākyamuni Buddha is not the only buddha; in Hakuin Zenji's *Zazen*

Wasan we read: "Sentient beings are primarily all buddhas." To this can be added—not just sentient beings; all beings, animate and inanimate, are enlightened ones. There is also the traditional Buddhist doctrine of the *Trikāya,* or "Three Bodies of Buddha." This refers to the Buddha's three principal metaphysical conditions: as the altogether formless Dharmakāya, or ultimate reality itself (in the Zen tradition known as Buddha-nature or *Mu*); as the Sambhogakāya, the form in which Buddha appears to preach to bodhisattvas; and the Nirmāṇakāya, the infinitely many concrete manifestations of the Buddha in accordance with the needs of sentient beings. (Sākyamuni Buddha can be spoken of as a Nirmāṇakāya Buddha.) Buddha can also be viewed from the point of view of the Three Treasures, the others being Dharma and Sangha.

BUDDHA-HRIDAYA Buddha's Mind, as opposed to Buddha's Words. See Nyogen Senzaki's article on p. 67 in this volume, "Buddha's Words, Buddha's Mind." Zen masters are masters of Buddha-Hridaya.

BUDDHA-WACCHANA Buddha's Words; the scriptures attributed to Buddha Sākyamuni.

DAZU HUIKE (487–593) (Daiso Eka, J.) The second patriarch of Zen (Chan) in China, and Bodhidharma's most famous successor. He is said to have cut off his arm while standing in the snow as an expression of his determination to realize his True Nature.

DHARMA NAME A name given, customarily in the Precepts ceremony, to a student who actualizes in everyday life the teachings of true Dharma.

DHARMAKĀYA The formless form of the Dharma; the condition of the Buddha as identical with ultimate reality itself. There are many Zen kōans regarding this matter; the most famous one is Master Jōshū's *Mu* (*Mumonkan, The Gateless Gate*, Case One).

DHYĀNA The original Sanskrit term from which the Japanese word Zen derives, by way of transliteration from the Chinese Chan. Dhyāna refers to contemplative discipline generally, and is the fifth of the Six Pāramitās. It is one of the three essential elements of all Buddhist practice (śīla, precepts; dhyāna, meditation; and prajñā, wisdom).

DIAMOND SŪTRA Known in Sanskrit as the Vajracchedika Prajñā-pāramitā Sūtra (Kongō Kyō, J.), it is one of the two most important sūtras of the Prajñāpāramitā literature (the Heart Sūtra is the other). The work took its present form in the fourth century; its essential doctrine that all things are "empty" or "void" (Śūnyatā) is a fundamental Buddhist teaching.

DŌGEN KIGEN (1200–53) The founder of the Sōtō school of Zen Buddhism in Japan and author of the *Shōbōgenzō*. A disciple of Myōan Eisai, Dōgen Zenji went to China in 1223, and stayed until 1227, studying under Master Tendō Nyojō (Tiantong Rujing, Ch.). On his return to Japan, he founded Eihei-Ji.

ECKHARDT, JOHANNES (1260–1328) Known as "Meister Eckhardt," this great Christian mystic and scholastic was a member of the Dominican Order. He was accused of heresy before a tribunal of the Franciscan-controlled Inquisition and was condemned posthumously. His student Johann Tauler, one of the leaders of the mystical society known as the "Friends of God," was largely responsible for the preservation of Meister Eckhardt's teachings. Eckhardt's writings are frequently quoted by modern Zen masters.

ENGAKU-JI One of the headquarters of Rinzai Zen in Japan, located in Kamakura and founded by Mugaku Sogen in 1282. Sōyen Shaku, D.T. Suzuki, and Nyogen Senzaki all practiced there.

ENGI-RON Nyogen Senzaki defines this as "Buddhist phenomenalism" (*jissō-ron* as "Buddhist ontology"). *Engi* means "arising from causation." *Engi-ron* may also be defined as the doctrine of causal production.

ESOTERIC BUDDHISM Called the "secret" or "hidden" teaching because it maintains that ultimate reality can be revealed only through mystical forms of action, speech, and thought. It developed in India during the seventh and eighth centuries, was transmitted to Tibet and China, and then to Japan, where it is known as Shingon Buddhism.

EXOTERIC BUDDHISM Contrasted to esoteric Buddhism, it is the belief that ultimate reality is already revealed and is neither secret nor hidden. This reality cannot be further explained; there is nothing to seek. It is just like water that cannot become wetter than it is. Exoteric Buddhists believe that Buddha's teaching has been written down clearly in words and phrases; therefore, esoteric devices are unnecessary.

GĀTHA A poem or chanted verse produced by a mind in a condition of spiritual insight. It is common in Zen Buddhism for the verbal expression of an enlightenment experience to take the gātha form.

HAIKU A Japanese verse form of seventeen syllables, usually arranged in lines of five, seven, and five. Essential to haiku is the appearance of a *kidai* or "season-word." Perhaps the greatest haiku master was Matsuo Bashō (1644–94). R. H. Blyth has said that haiku is an expression of enlightenment, a seeing into the life of things. See his four-volume

Haiku, as well as his *Zen in English Literature.* Also recommended is D.T. Suzuki's *Zen and Japanese Culture.*

HAKUIN EKAKU (1685–1768) The towering Zen master who revived Rinzai Zen in Japan after its period of decline in the eighteenth century. Hakuin Zenji is responsible for the complete remodeling of the Rinzai kōan system and was the honorary founder of Ryūtaku-Ji. Author of the important *Zazen Wasan* (Song of Zazen), his writings appear in English translation in Philip Yampolsky's *The Zen Master Hakuin* and R.D.M. Shaw's *The Embossed Tea Kettle.* His was an astonishingly diverse genius, which expressed itself in many forms, including teaching, writing, and painting. It is said that a master of his caliber appears only once every five hundred years.

HEKIGAN ROKU Known as *The Blue Cliff Record* or *The Blue Rock Collection,* this is one of the most important texts in Rinzai Zen Buddhism. It consists of a hundred kōans compiled by Zen master Setchō Jūshin with verse commentary by him, and was called *Setchō's Hundred Kōans and Verse Commentary.* Later another Zen master, Engo Kokugon, wrote an introduction to each kōan as well as a short phrase-by-phrase commentary on both the kōans and Setchō's verses. This was followed by his own comments on each case. The room where Engo worked had a plaque with the words *Heki Gan* (Blue Cliff) inscribed on it; thus he gave this collection its name. The *Hekigan Roku* was completed in 1125 and was brought to Japan in the thirteenth century. In the Sōtō tradition, the parallel text would be the *Shōyō Roku (The Book of Equanimity).*

HINAYĀNA BUDDHISM Literally "Lesser Vehicle." This term was coined by Mahāyāna Buddhists to refer in a somewhat disparaging manner to the more conservative and doctrinaire nature of what is more properly spoken of as Theravāda Buddhism ("The tradition of the

Elders"). "Lesser Vehicle" means that according to the teaching of this school, it is not possible for all beings to become enlightened. The Mahāyāna position—that of the "Great Vehicle"—is that in principle all beings can "attain" emancipation. The Hinayāna is also associated with the Two Vehicles, the śrāvakayāna and the pratyeka-buddhayāna. (See Theravāda and Mahāyāna.)

HYAKUJŌ EKAI (720–814) (Baizhang Huaihai, Ch.) One of the great Chinese Zen masters of the Tang period; a student and successor of Baso Dōitsu (Mazu Daoyi, Ch.) and the master of Isan Reiyū (Guishan Lingyou, Ch.) and Ōbaku Kiun (Huangbo Xiyun, Ch.). Hyakujō founded the Zen monastic tradition by establishing precise rules for the life and daily routine of a monastery. He is famous for the saying, "A day without work, a day without food."

IKEBANA The art of Japanese flower arrangement. The "art" lies not in arranging the flowers, but in learning how to allow them to arrange themselves.

JAKUSHITSU GENKŌ (1289–1367) A Zen master and poet of fourteenth-century Japan. He went to China in 1319, remaining there for six years before returning to Japan where, in 1361, he established Eigen-Ji. His most famous work is the *Jakushitsu Goroku.*

JISSŌ-RON Nyogen Senzaki defines this as "Buddhist ontology" as contrasted to engi-ron or "Buddhist phenomenalism." Jissō-ron is usually associated with the Tendai school, and the engi-ron teachings with the Kegon school. Literally *jissō* means "real or true form" and *ron* means "the theory of." Jissō-ron explains the being of things; engi-ron, their phenomenal existence.

JŌSHŪ JŪSHIN (778–897) The great Zen master of the Tang Dynasty in China (Zhaozhou Dongshen, Ch.), who attained his first kenshō at the age of eighteen and complete enlightenment at fifty-four. He did not begin formal teaching until he had completed his pilgrimages at the age of eighty. He is said to have died at the age of 120. The Dharma heir of Nansen Fugan (Nanquan Puyuan, Ch.), he is best known in the West as the originator of the *Mu* kōan. His Zen is called *kushimpi,* which literally means "comes from the lips"; that is, only a few words from his mouth were needed to express his teaching, so profound was his maturity and so gentle was his manner. Almost all of the kōans associated with him are characterized by directness, forcefulness, and brevity of expression. His most famous kōans—in addition to *Mu*— are "Have a Cup of Tea" and "The Cypress Tree in the Garden."

KANZAN A well-known Zen figure of the Tang Dynasty, Kanzan (Hanshan, Ch.) was a great sage, whose behavior was notoriously eccentric. His Zen poetry is highly regarded. He disappeared mysteriously, and later generations held him to be an avatar of Mañjuśrī Bodhisattva.

KARMA Literally "action." Karma is usually identified with the law of cause and effect as it operates in the moral and the physical domain. But in a broader sense everything *is* karma itself. Karma is not limited by time and space, nor is it something exclusively individual; there is also collective karma. The three sources of karma are said to be body, mouth, and thought. Associated with karma is the idea of the continuity of life and death. In the deepest sense, karma is energy, and as the modern physical principle states, matter cannot be destroyed, but must be conserved as energy. Therefore, although a given physical manifestation may disintegrate, the energy itself cannot be destroyed, but returns in a different manifestation in accordance with circumstances. The Western concept of fate and the basically Eastern notion of karma are not at all the same. One's karma can be changed by one's own actions. See Nyogen Senzaki's "Karma" (p. 88) as well as "Karma, Ālaya, and Tathatā" (p. 90); also D.T. Suzuki's discussion of karma and no-karma in *The Essence of Buddhism* and Hakuun Yasutani Rōshi's *The Eight Beliefs of Buddhism.*

KENSHŌ Also called satori, kenshō is considered essential to Rinzai Zen practice. Literally *ken* means "seeing into" and *shō* means "one's own nature." This occurs when one has broken through all one's preconceptions and has wiped away the dust covering the Mind-Mirror. There are two contributing causes of kenshō: accumulated samādhi and what is known as "karma-relation"—something that triggers the experience.

KŌAN An abbreviation of *kōfu no andoku* (the "kō" and "an" having been put together to form one word). *Kōfu* means "public" and *andoku* means "document"; hence the implication of something reliable because non-subjective. A kōan is a Zen dialogue found in one of several Zen texts. It is said that about 1,700 such kōans exist. However, in a broader sense, everyday life itself is a kōan (the *genjō kōan* of the Sōtō Zen tradition). In the Rinzai school, kōans are used as a method of concentration during zazen; through intense unification with one's kōan, one polishes one's understanding. Particularly valuable is the book by Miura Isshū Rōshi and Ruth Fuller Sasaki, *Zen Dust.* (Though that version is long out of print, a shorter version of this has appeared under the title of *The Zen Kōan.*)

MAHĀKASHAPA Buddha Sākyamuni's successor and the senior disciple who headed the First Council after Buddha's death. In the *Mumonkan (The Gateless Gate)* there is a well-known kōan associated with him (Case Six, "The Buddha's Flower").

MAHĀPRAJÑĀPĀRAMITĀ SŪTRA Known as the Heart Sūtra (Hannyashin Gyō, J.). Commonly considered a condensation of the essence (heart) of the Prajñāpāramitā literature. (Kōbō Daishi Kūkai disagreed, however, arguing that it is an independent sūtra.) Along with the Diamond Sūtra, the Heart Sūtra is the most important and most frequently recited sūtra of the Prajñāpāramitā class. It is the only sūtra chanted by almost all Buddhist schools in Japan; one exception is the Shin Buddhist school.

MAHĀYĀNA Literally the "Great Vehicle." Its essence is a progressive and liberal spirit, which seeks, without contradicting the original teachings of the Buddha, to broaden their scope and usefulness. In the words of D.T. Suzuki *(Outlines of Mahāyāna Buddhism),* this form of Buddhism is "a boundless ocean in which all forms of thought and faith can find their congenial and welcome home." According to the Mahāyāna teaching, all beings are primarily buddhas and can realize this in their own lifetime. The Mahāyāna is associated with the third of the Three Vehicles, the bodhisattvayāna. (See Theravāda.)

MANAS According to the Vijñāna System, manas *(manashiki,* J.) is the seventh of the eight consciousnesses and is the source of dualistic self-awareness. It conveys to the ālaya what has been received from the first six consciousnesses and, as a result of a misapprehension of ālaya's true nature, generates the delusion of a permanent ego. (See Ālaya and Vijñāna.)

MANDALA A consecrated geometrical representation whose symbolism is designed to provide unification with the forces of the universe. The use of such symbolism is primarily associated with Tibetan and Shingon Buddhism. (See Nyogen Senzaki's talk "Esoteric Buddhism" on p. 126 for an account of the relation between mandala meditation and Zen practice.)

MAYA The name of Buddha Sākyamuni's mother. Maya also means illusion, as well as the medium through which the phenomenal world is apprehended.

MU Although the literal meaning is that of a negative syllable ("no" or "nothing"), *Mu* is usually used in a more positive sense, as for example in the famous kōan known as "Jōshū's Dog" (Case One of the *Mumonkan*): "A monk asked Jōshū: 'Does a dog have Buddha-nature or not?' Jōshū answered: "*Mu!*" *Mu* is none other than our own Mind, the formless form of the Dharma.

NAMO TASSO BHAGAVATO ARAHATO SAMMA SAMBUDDHASSA "Homage to Him, the Holy One, the Enlightened One, the Supremely Awakened One."

NIRVĀṆA Literally "extinction," both in the active and passive senses. When the fires of delusion have been blown out, the fact of original enlightenment reveals itself. Nirvāṇa is not an abstract concept, nor some distant heaven; although often understood in a negative way as synonymous with quiescence, it has a positive, dynamic meaning, and can be experienced in one's own lifetime. Nirvāṇa is not to be confused with Parinirvāṇa (the Buddha Sākyamuni's death). According to the Mahāyāna view, nirvāṇa is a condition analogous to the deepest samādhi, and is seen as having four essential qualities, expressed in the Japanese as *jō raku ga jō,* meaning "eternal, joyous, selfless, and pure."

NOUMENON This technical term in Western philosophy—used in contrast with "phenomenon"—was coined by the German philosopher Immanuel Kant. Literally "thing of reason," it connotes that which enjoys an absolute—because mind-created—existence. Nyogen

Senzaki uses this term frequently in an attempt to render the notion of the absolute in Western terms.

NYOI A staff or stick used by Zen masters. The word literally means "according to the mind," and this is the way it is used by them—sometimes as a keisaku, sometimes in more ceremonial contexts. It is made either of iron or wood, and usually is about a foot and a half in length.

OX HERDING PICTURES A series of ten (sometimes six) pictures with poetic commentary depicting the stages of Zen practice. Created by Kakuan Shien (Kuoan Shiyuan, Ch.), a master of the Sung Dynasty in China. The stages are: searching for the ox (our True Nature); finding the footprints; seeing the ox in the distance; catching the ox; becoming intimate with it; riding home; forgetting the ox; both person and ox forgotten; returning to one's origin before the search (everything is different but the same); and returning to ordinary life, one's feet on the ground, one's spirit in heaven. Among the works in English that contain this series are: Philip Kapleau's *The Three Pillars of Zen*, Nyogen Senzaki and Paul Reps's *Zen Flesh, Zen Bones*, D.T. Suzuki's *Manual of Zen Buddhism* and First Series of *Essays in Zen Buddhism*, and Shibayama Zenkei's *A Flower Does Not Talk*.

PĀRAMITĀS *Pāramitā* means "to reach the other shore." The pāramitās are the virtues of perfection, which are: charity (*dāna*, Skt.), keeping the precepts (*śīla*, Skt.), patience or endurance (*kshānti*, Skt.), diligence (*virya*, Skt.), meditative absorption (*dhyāna*, Skt.), and wisdom (*prajñā*, Skt.). The practice of these virtues is characteristic of the bodhisattva. By observing them we realize that the other shore is not the other shore, but is right here, right now. These virtues are in fact concrete methods by which this realization can be attained.

PATRIARCH In the most narrow sense "Patriarch" (*soshi*, J.) refers to Bodhidharma. In a slightly broader sense, it means any Zen master up to Huineng, the sixth patriarch in China. In an even broader sense, however, it includes all Zen masters past, present, and future; and, moreover, not only Zen masters but enlightened teachers of other schools and traditions as well.

PHENOMENON Used in a technical sense in contrast to "noumenon," it refers to mere relative existence.

PRAGMATISM The American philosophy originated by Charles Sanders Peirce and associated with the work of William James and John Dewey. On a popular level, pragmatism (to paraphrase James) is the belief that something is true if it works. On a deeper level, it is the insistence on the unity of theory and practice. Zen is related to pragmatism in both senses. This similarity has been noted by many modern Zen masters in this country.

PRAJÑĀ Perhaps the single most important idea in Zen Buddhism, prajñā (*hannya,* J.) is the core of the Prajñāpāramitā literature. It means "wisdom" or "intuitive insight" and is the sixth pāramitā. Its relationship to dhyāna, the fifth pāramitā, is crucial. Zen practice is based on the inseparability of the two, which is revealed in zazen-samādhi. Since Huineng, this inseparability has been strongly emphasized. See D.T. Suzuki's *The Zen Doctrine of No-Mind,* pp. 45–49, and *Essays in Zen Buddhism,* Third Series, pp. 243–94 ("The Philosophy of the Prajñāpāramitā").

PRAJÑĀPĀRAMITĀ The perfection of wisdom; literally "the wisdom that leads to the other shore."

PRATYEKABUDDHA In Japanese, *engaku. En* means "karmic connection" and *gaku* means "enlightened." Hence the meaning of "self-enlightened Buddha," or one who attains enlightenment without a teacher. As contrasted to the bodhisattva, the pratyekabuddha chooses a solitary existence, neither preaching the Dharma nor helping others to attain emancipation. Hence, the pratyekabuddha is one whose enlightenment results from an understanding of karmic connection (known in Buddhism as the Pratītyasamutpāda, the "twelvefold chain of dependent origination").

RINZAI GIGEN (?–867) (Linji, Ch.) The great Chinese Zen master of the Tang Dynasty; the founder of the Rinzai school of Zen Buddhism whose teachings were compiled into the *Rinzai Roku (The Sayings of Master Rinzai)*. The Rinzai school was one of five Zen schools in the Tang Dynasty; the four others were the Sōtō, Unmon, Igyō, and Hōgen. Rinzai Zenji was the successor of Huangbo (Ōbaku. J.)

RŌSHI Literally "elder teacher." A rōshi is a Zen master who has received inka (Dharma acknowledgment) from his or her master. Essential to this transmission is the master's estimation of the student's maturity and readiness. Contrary to popular belief, the completion of the traditional kōan study does not automatically mean that one is a rōshi. Like the pouring of water from one cup to another, this transmission of Dharma from mind to mind is uniquely Zen in character. It usually takes at least twenty years of Zen training before the title of rōshi is conferred in the Rinzai tradition. There are rare and exceptional cases—Nyogen Senzaki, for example—of people who are truly rōshis even though they have no such title. One of the ways in which the Rinzai and Sōtō schools differ is in the bestowing of inka.

RŪPA Form as contrasted with formlessness.

SADDHARMA-PUNDARĪKA SŪTRA The Lotus Sūtra (Myōhō Renge Kyō, or Hoke Kyō, J.) was written in the second century in India, and consists of twenty-eight chapters (the twenty-fifth being the famous Kannon Sūtra). One of the most important Mahāyāna Buddhist scriptures, in it the characteristic Mahāyāna view that the Buddha is in essence trans-historical is first asserted. According to this interpretation, the Buddha's manifestation as a human being in the phenomenal world is ultimately a matter of upāya (skillful means). The Lotus Sūtra also teaches that even those adhering to the so-called Lesser Vehicle can attain perfect enlightenment.

SAMĀDHI In Japanese, *samādhi* is translated as *shōju,* which means "right receiving." (The transliteration in Japanese is *zammai.*) Only when one has entered into samādhi can one receive things as they are; for in such a condition the mind is clear and lucid, free from impurities and impediments. See Nyogen Senzaki's "The Meaning of Sesshin" (p. 110) in this volume.

SAMSĀRA The relative, phenomenal world of ceaseless becoming and suffering. The Japanese translation *shōji* literally means "birth-death." Another meaning of *shōji* is "distracting thoughts." Even in the midst of distracting thoughts, there is enlightenment. This is a concrete way of expressing the well-known but mysterious identification of samsāra and nirvāna in Mahāyāna Buddhism. It is characteristic of the Theravāda tradition to separate samsāra and nirvāna.

SAṄGHA One of the Three Treasures of Buddhism, along with Buddha and Dharma. The original meaning is the historical assembly of monks and nuns surrounding Buddha Sākyamuni, but it is usually used in a broader sense to refer to any group of students of Buddhism united by their common practice. Saṅgha, like the other two Treasures, can be viewed from three distinct but related vantage points:

the historical, the practical, and the philosophical. See Nyogen Senzaki's "The Three Treasures" (p. 112).

SELF-NATURE As Hakuin Zenji says in his *Zazen Wasan:* "If we concentrate within and testify to the truth that self-nature is no-nature, we have really gone beyond foolish talk." The intuitive realization that self-nature is no-nature and no-nature is self-nature is the experience of *kenshō.* To say that self-nature is no-nature means that all beings are transformations in accordance with differing causal conditions. The law of causation undermines any attempt to establish immutable being in the world, and underlies the Buddhist doctrine of anātta (selflessness).

SESSHIN Literally "to collect the mind." Sesshin is the Buddhist seclusion or retreat, consisting of seven days of intensive zazen practice, with teishō by the rōshi and dokusan a few times a day. During sesshin, students concentrate on nothing but collecting the scattered mind so that they can realize their original unity with the universe from which they ordinarily feel separated. In Japanese monasteries, sesshin is held six or seven times a year. See Nyogen Senzaki's "The Meaning of Sesshin" (p. 110).

SHIN In Eastern philosophy and religion, "Mind" is conceived of in non-psychological terms and refers to ultimate reality itself. The purpose of zazen is nothing but the realization of this Mind. See D.T. Suzuki on the meaning of *shin* in *Manual of Zen Buddhism.*

SHINGON Literally "true word," a translation of the Sanskrit mantra, which refers to secret formulae and mystical doctrines that cannot be expressed in ordinary words. The name indicates the importance attributed to speech, which Shingon Buddhism considers one of the Three Mysteries (the other two are the mysteries of body and mind).

Shingon teaching is only for the initiated, not for the public, and the relation between teacher and student is all important. Kōbō Daishi Kūkai (774–835) was the founder of this school of Buddhism in Japan. Because of the importance of mantras in Shingon, it is often referred to as the "Mantrayāna."

SHINNYO The truth which pervades the whole universe; sometimes called Dharma-nature or Buddha-nature. *Shin* means "truth [without falsehood]" and *nyo* means "the unchangeable nature [of this truth]."

SHŌBŌGENZŌ The ninety-five-fascicle work written by Dōgen Kigen Zenji, who introduced the Sōtō school of Zen from China to Japan. The *Shōbōgenzō* is this school's central text (as is the *Rinzai Roku* for the Rinzai school). *Shōbō* means "True Dharma"; *genzō* means "Treasure Eye."

SHŌYŌ ROKU Known in English as *The Book of Equanimity.* A collection of one hundred Zen dialogues with verses compiled by Wanshi Shō-gaku (1090–1157) of the Sōtō school. Banshō Gyōshu (1165–1246) added his own commentary. This is one of the most important texts in Sōtō Zen Buddhism. The equivalent in the Rinzai tradition would be the *Hekigan Roku (The Blue Cliff Collection).*

ŚĪLA With dhyāna and prajñā, a cornerstone of Buddhist theory and practice. Śīla is the ethical or moral foundation of Buddhism. It refers specifically to the keeping of the precepts, but in a broader sense it is concerned with appropriate behavior. Śīla is the precondition of right concentration (dhyāna), which in turn is inseparable from and a necessary condition for the realization of true wisdom (prajñā).

SKANDHAS Known as "the five aggregates," or the five causally conditioned elements of existence. All phenomena in the world are classifiable in terms of these aggregates which are: rūpa (form), vedana (feeling), samjñā (thought), samskara (volition/discrimination), and vijñāna (perception/consciousness).

SŌTŌ ZEN One of the five schools of Zen Buddhism which originated in China during the Tang Dynasty. Its founders were masters Sōzan Honjaku (Caoshan Benji, Ch.) and Tōzan Ryōkai (Dongshan Liangjie, Ch.) and it was brought to Japan by Eihei Dōgen Kigen. Sōtō Zen, which is also called Mokushō ("silent illumination") Zen, as contrasted to Kanna (Kōan) Zen, stresses *shikan taza* practice and original enlightenment (*honrai jōbutsu,* J.). Rinzai Zen emphasizes the necessity of the experience of enlightenment (*kenshō jōbutsu,* J.), which is nothing but the realization that we are enlightened from the very beginning. In the Sōtō school, zazen is seen as the revelation of original enlightenment; in the Rinzai tradition, even though it is acknowledged that all beings are primarily buddhas, kenshō is considered indispensable. Sōtō and Rinzai are the two dominant Zen schools in modern-day Japan and America.

ŚRĀVAKA Literally a "hearer." A direct disciple of Buddha Śākyamuni who, having heard and received his teaching, seeks his own salvation. Usually contrasted with the pratyekabuddha and the bodhisattva.

SUFISM A form of Moslem mysticism which has been informally referred to as "Mohammedan Zen."

SŪTRA Literally means "scripture." The term refers either to an individual scripture or to the section of the Tripiṭaka containing the dialogues and discourses attributed to the historical Buddha. The other two sections are the Shastra and the Vinaya. Although attributed to the historical Buddha Sākyamuni (especially by Theravādins), many sūtras were not in fact delivered by him, but were written considerably later. In general, the Mahāyāna tradition does not view sūtras from a literalistic or fundamentalist point of view.

TAKUHATSU The traditional practice in which monks, wearing wide circular straw hats that limit their vision, walk through a town chanting *Hō* (Dharma) and receive offerings. Monk and donor bow to each other at the same time. This practice is not begging, but an "exchange" of the spiritual and the material.

TATHĀGATA One of the ten epithets of the Buddha used not only by his followers but also applied by him to himself, which gives it a special significance. There is some controversy as to the exact derivation of the term. Some claim it derives from "thus come," while others argue that it comes from "thus gone." Because the idea of the Buddha coming and/or going is inimical to the absolutist spirit of Zen, instead of interpreting this expression in this manner, Zen tends rather to locate Buddha where there is neither coming nor going—in the region of true suchness. In the words of Hakuin Zenji in "The Song of Zazen": "Whether going or returning / we cannot be any place else." In the Mahāyāna-Zen tradition, Tathāgata is identified with Tathatā (Suchness).

TATHATĀ The Mahāyāna expression meaning "Suchness" or "Thusness." The positive side of śūnyatā, Tathatā means that ultimate reality is beyond affirmation and negation—it is *as it is.*

TEISHŌ *Tei* literally means "to carry" and *shō* means "to declare." In a teishō the rōshi tries in an immediate, concrete, and vivid way to show Buddha-Dharma without resorting to any of the myriad devices and crutches of conceptualization. Normally this special form of Zen presentation takes place during sesshin and uses traditional Zen texts such as the *Rinzai Roku, Hekigan Roku,* or *Mumonkan.*

TENDAI A school of Buddhism originating in India and founded by Hui-wen (550–77) in China as a result of the influence of Nāgārjuna's thought. There is both a Chinese (Tiantai) and a Japanese Tendai sect. The Japanese school was founded by Dengyō Daishi Saichō in 805. The Saddharma-pundarīka Sūtra (the Lotus Sūtra) is its principal teaching. The Japanese Tendai school includes doctrines of esoteric Buddhism, as well as a Zen-influenced meditation practice known as *makashikan.*

TENZO The cook-monk in a Zen monastery. Normally a senior student is given this important responsibility.

THEOSOPHICAL SOCIETY A highly eclectic and esoteric organization whose goals are: universal brotherhood, the study of comparative religion, philosophy, and science, and the investigation of the laws of nature as well as the powers latent in humankind. Associated with the name of Madame Helena Petrovna Blavatsky, one of its founders.

THERAVĀDA Literally "doctrine of the Elders." One of the two mainstreams of Buddhism; considered to be the orthodox form because its scriptures are in the original Pāli language. Characterized by the Two Vehicles of the śrāvaka and the pratyekabuddha, the Theravāda tradition is maintained in the countries of Sri Lanka, Vietnam, Thailand, Laos, Bangladesh, and Cambodia; for this reason, it is sometimes referred to as the Southern School (Mahāyāna Buddhism is found in the northern countries of China, Japan, Korea, and Tibet). (See Hinayāna Buddhism.)

TRIPIṬAKA Literally "three boxes, or baskets." A collection of works constituting the Pāli Buddhist Canon, whose three parts are Sūtra (Buddha's teachings), Shastra (commentaries on the sūtras), and Vinaya (Buddha's commandments).

TRIRATNA Literally "Three Treasures," the foundation of Buddhist life: Buddha, Dharma, and Saṅgha. These treasures can be interpreted in three different ways: the philosophical, the practical, and the historical. See Nyogen Senzaki's "The Three Treasures" (p. 112). For an account of these Treasures in the context of modern Buddhism, see Saṅgharakṣita's *The Three Jewels*.

UNMON BUN-EN (?–949) (Yunmen Wenyan, Ch.) The founder of the Unmon school, one of the five schools of Zen Buddhism during the Tang Dynasty. His name comes from the fact that he lived on Mount Unmon. The successor of Seppō Gison (Xuefeng Yicun, Ch.), his teaching was characterized by extremely pithy, pointed, and vital responses to students' questions; the verbal expression of Unmon was always at the same time both elegant and poetic. He is considered one of the great Zen masters of all time. Many kōans have been attributed to him; one of the most famous is "Every day is a good day."

UPĀSAKA, UPĀSIKĀ Laymen and laywomen disciples in Buddhism, respectively.

UPĀYA Literally "skillful means." When the Buddha began teaching, he is said to have realized that it would not be possible for him to reveal the Dharma as it is to all beings, because of differences in capacity and readiness. Accordingly, he formulated upāya which would enable him to teach all beings in accordance with their circumstances. Such skillful means are expressions of the effective cooperation of prajñā (wisdom) and karuna (love). The Japanese have a saying, *Uso mo hōben* ("Sometimes even telling a lie can be skillful means!").

UTA Another name for a *waka,* a thirty-one syllable Japanese poem, sometimes expressed in song.

VAJRADHĀTU (*Kongōkai,* J.) Together with the Garbha-kośa-dhātu, one of the two basic mandala forms. Known as the mandala of subjectivity, or the "Diamond Cutter," it symbolizes the crushing of delusion.

VEDANTA One of six orthodox systems of Indian philosophy; the consummation of the doctrine of the Vedas as set forth in the *Upanisads.* Its chief exponent was Saṃskāra, ca. 800. Essentially Vedanta is a philosophy of non-dualism. That it is a philosophy, not a religion in the usual sense of the term, should be emphasized. It was introduced into this country by Swami Vivekananda at the same time as Zen Buddhism—in 1893, at the World's Parliament of Religions in Chicago.

VESAK (VESHAKA) (*Vesak,* Skt., *Wesak,* Pali) The full-moon night of the fourth lunar month on which is celebrated the birth, renunciation, enlightenment, and Parinirvāṇa of Buddha Sākyamuni. This is basically a Theravāda or Southern Buddhist festival, but the all-pervading, universal light of the full moon transcends distinctions between Theravāda and Mahāyāna, Buddhist and non-Buddhist.

VIJÑĀNA Consciousness. Used as a suffix (e.g., ālayavijñāna), it refers to a specific consciousness, in accordance with a classificatory scheme known as the "Vijñāna System," which is associated with the Yogācāra school of Buddhism. (See Ālaya and Manas.)

WAKA A thirty-one-syllable Japanese poem.

WHEEL OF DHARMA Turning or revolving the Wheel of Dharma is a metaphorical reference to the Buddha Sākyamuni's First Sermon in the Deer Park at Sarnath near Benares. However, Dharma activity of *any* kind can be considered to be a turning of this Wheel.

WORLD'S PARLIAMENT OF RELIGIONS, THE Held at the Columbian Exposition in Chicago in 1893. A historical event of considerable significance, in many ways it marked the real beginning of the movement of Eastern religion and philosophy into American culture. In addition to Sōyen Shaku Rōshi, also present was the famous Vedanta master Swami Vivekananda.

ZAZEN Literally "sitting Zen." Although it can be interpreted in a broader sense, strictly speaking, zazen is the practice in which, sitting cross-legged on a cushion, one regulates one's breathing, disciplines one's mind, and enters into an experience of one's original unity with all things. Sometimes referred to as "Zen meditation," zazen should not be considered meditation, at least not in the sense the term is generally used. The heart of the practice of Zen Buddhism, zazen is both a means to the attainment of enlightenment as well as a manifestation of original enlightenment: both something one does and something one is. Zazen practice is based on the inseparability of dhyāna and prajñā, and is devoted to the single-minded integration of bodhisattva spirit in one's everyday life.

ZEN The Japanese transliteration of the Sanskrit dhyāna (by way of a transliteration of the Chinese Chan). However, Zen does not mean the same as dhyāna. The essence of Zen is the unity of dhyāna and prajñā; in practice, this union is none other than zazen-samādhi. The Indian practice of dhyāna has a more metaphysical nature, while what is known nowadays as Zen has a much more practical, feet-on-the-ground character. Although generally considered one school of

Buddhism among many, in a broader sense Zen is the heart of Buddhism, as well as another name for all religions, all culture, and for Mind itself. This heart of all things is the Mind Buddha Sākyamuni realized and transmitted to his successor, the seal of the Bodhicitta (Buddha-Mind) that has been transmitted in the Zen tradition century after century.

ZENDO The place where formal zazen is practiced.

ZENJI *Ji* is written with two different characters. The first means "teacher." In this sense *Zenji* means "Zen teacher or Zen master." The second means "samurai," implying "fellow" or "person." Here Zenji is roughly the same as *unsui*—that is, "a monk practicing in a monastery." In America, however, the term is most often used in contrast to *Koji* ("layman"), and in referring to a Zen master in the past (e.g., Hakuin Ekaku Zenji).

Notes

CHINESE POEMS

1 Lucifer is the planet Venus seen as the morning star; Vesper, the same planet seen as the evening star.
2 Shūbin Tanahashi was Nyogen Senzaki's first student. For details see Eidō Shimano Rōshi's Introduction, p. 1.
3 Heart Mountain (Wyoming) was the location of the internment camp that Nyogen Senzaki was sent to when war broke out in 1941. For details see Eidō Shimano Rōshi's Introduction, p. 1.

DHARMA TALKS

1 "Mentorgarten movement" can mean: a) Nyogen Senzaki's own vision or interpretation of Buddhism; b) the community or Saṅgha he founded in Japan around 1901 and continued in spirit in America, first in San Francisco around the 1920s and c) then in Los Angeles, at the Mentorgarten Zendo from the 1930s on.
2 Friedrich Froebel (1782–1852) was a German educational reformer and founder of the kindergarten system.
3 This is an allusion to Kant's famous dictum "Concepts without percepts are empty; percepts without concepts are blind."
4 About his "awkward English" Nyogen Senzaki once wrote this poem, which he dedicated to his student and editor, Ruth Strout McCandless, whose Dharma name was Kangetsu:

> My English writings
> Have too many rips and rents.
> Who else can stitch and mend
> Except the old friend, Kangetsu?
> (January 16, 1946)

5 D.T. Suzuki, *An Introduction to Zen Buddhism* (New York: Causeway Books, 1974), p. 39. The quotation may have originally appeared in an article with the title mentioned, but in this volume it is part of a chapter entitled "What Is Zen?"
6 Twelfth-century Scottish monk and prior of the Abbey of St. Victor in Paris.
7 This is a bit difficult to follow. The "real" squash is the squash as inseparable from all other things in the universe. This condition of inseparability requires a transcendence of perception in the direction of pure conception. In brief: The real squash is not squash, but the whole universe.

8 Bodhidharma's successor, Dazu Huike (Daisa Eka, J.), the second patriarch of Zen in China.

9 Case #18 of the *Blue Cliff Record.*

10 The etymology of the word "utopia" is of particular importance here. It means literally "nowhere" or "no-place." To be "nowhere" in a slightly extended sense of the word, then, is to be beyond time and place—"absolutely" nowhere. Samuel Butler's *Erewhon,* a satire on utopian thinking, plays on this same etymology: The title is essentially "nowhere" spelled backward.

11 D.T. Suzuki, *Essays in Zen Buddhism,* First Series (London: Rider and Company, 1970), p. 22.

12 This is Nyogen Senzaki's title but it appears in the manuscript with a line drawn through it.

13 D.T. Suzuki, *Manual of Zen Buddhism* (London: Rider and Company, 1957), p. 76. This comes in a note to "On Believing in Mind" (Shinjinmei), a classic Zen text.

14 These "pictured fans" illustrate the first three stages of Zen training and are based on the traditional "Oxherding" series. For more on this, see the Glossary.

15 Franz Kafka once said: "We are sinful not merely because we have eaten of the Tree of Knowledge, but also because we have not yet eaten of the Tree of Life. The state in which we find ourselves is sinful, quite independent of guilt." Franz Kafka, *The Great Wall of China* (New York: Schocken Books, 1970), p. 178.

16 While Nyogen Senzaki was in the concentration camp on Heart Mountain in Wyoming, he whiled away his time working on his version—by his own admission somewhat "playful"—of the classic Sōtō text, the *Shōyō Roku,* or *Book of Equanimity.* Nyogen Senzaki said of this project on May 12th, 1944 (in his own Introduction): "I am trying to renew the old meditation class in this peculiar way because I am living now within the barbed-wire fences of a relocation center for so-called Japs and so cannot be personally present to my students."

17 Nyogen Senzaki uses the German word *Ideologie* rather than the English "ideology" because of the subtle difference in connotation between the two. Although originally a French word, it has come to be associated with German usage because of the meaning given it by Karl Marx.

18 Sōyen Shaku, "The God-Conception of Buddhism" in *Zen for Americans* (La Salle, Illinois: Open Court, 1974), pp. 26, 29. The German scholar in the quote above is Rudolph Otto.

19 These mean, respectively: "I go to the Buddha for refuge"; "I go to the Dharma for refuge"; and "I go to the Saṅgha for refuge."

20 Everything here is by Nyogen Senzaki, except the very last paragraph, which is a brief eulogy by one of his students.

21 This quotation is from Nyogen Senzaki's will.

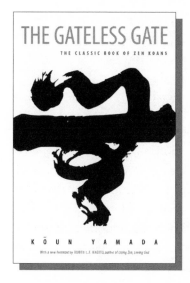

The Gateless Gate
The Classic Book of Zen Koans
Koun Yamada
Foreword by Ruben L.F. Habito
288 pages, ISBN 0-86171-382-6, $16.95

"Koun Yamada's superb translation of The Gateless Gate has accompanied me throughout my practice and my teaching ever since the first edition appeared over two decades ago. His teisho on the Cases are alive and pithy, directly conveying Master Mumon's vivid Zen and the life-transforming words of our ancestral teachers. How fortunate we are to have this new edition, with a Foreword by the esteemed Ruben Habito."—Roko Sherry Chayat, Abbot, Zen Center of Syracuse Hoen-ji

"The penetrating voice of a unique lay Zen master! The depth of Yamada Koun Roshi's insight doesn't allow him to keep any religious, cultural or racial border in his heart. Consequently many westerners as well as catholic fathers and sisters joined his sangha. Reading his words, we realize that the Dharma has nothing to do with east or west, Buddhism or Christiany. Buddha nature is universal."—Eido Shimano Roshi, Abbot of Dai Bosatsu Zendo, Kongo-Ji

"Koun Yamada Roshi's insightful and profound commentaries on the *Gateless Gate* will help Zen students of all abilities to appreciate the significance of koans, not as riddles, but as touchstones of reality."—Gerry Shishin Wick Roshi, author of *The Book of Equanimity*

Includes: An in-depth introduction to the history of Zen practice and lineage charts, Japanese-to-Chinese and Chinese-to-Japanese conversion charts for personal names, place names, and names of writings, plus, front- and back-matter from ancient and modern figures: Mumon, Shuan, Kubota Ji'un, Taizan Maezumi, Hugo Enomiya-Lasalle, and Yamada Roshi's son, Masamichi Yamada.

The Book of Equanimity
Illuminating Classic Zen Koans
Gerry Shishin Wick
Foreword by Bernie Glassman
320 pages, ISBN 0-86171-387-7, $19.95

Though it is one of the most beloved collections of koans, the *Shoyoroku* has never before been available with commentary from a contemporary Zen master. Here, Shishin Wick offers new translations of these classic koans, along with his concise original commentaries.

"Shishin Wick's commentaries on this timeless series of koans illuminate the ancient wisdom of the east for our modern scientific world. There are few today who could shed this kind of light for the Western reader in the 21st century."—Dennis Genpo Merzel, Roshi, President of the White Plum Asanga and Kanzeon International

"Gerry Shishin Wick is a Zen teacher of long experience and uncommon depth of practice. Every student of Zen would do well to read this fine book and anything else he writes."—Robert Jinsen Kennedy, author of *Zen Spirit, Christian Spirit*

"Wick's pithy commentaries on the *Book of Equanimity* cut to the quick of the one hundred cases contained in it... A beacon that penetrates through the haze of complications."—John Daido Loori, editor of *Sitting With Koans*

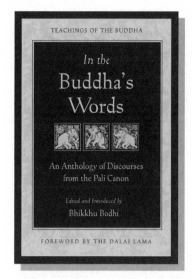

In the Buddha's Words
An Anthology of Discourses from the Pali Canon
Edited and introduced by Bhikkhu Bodhi
Foreword by the Dalai Lama
512 pages, ISBN 0-86171-491-1, $18.95

This landmark collection is the definitive introduction to the Buddha's teachings—in his own words. The American scholar-monk Bhikkhu Bodhi, whose voluminous translations have won widespread acclaim, here presents selected discourses of the Buddha from the Pāli Canon, the earliest record of what the Buddha taught. Divided into ten thematic chapters, *In the Buddha's Words* reveals the full scope of the Buddha's discourses, from family life and marriage to renunciation and the path of insight. A concise, informative introduction precedes each chapter, guiding the reader toward a deeper understanding of the texts that follow.

In the Buddha's Words allows even readers unacquainted with Buddhism to grasp the significance of the Buddha's contributions to our world heritage. Taken as a whole, these texts bear eloquent testimony to the breadth and intelligence of the Buddha's teachings, and point the way to an ancient yet ever-vital path. Students and seekers alike will find this systematic presentation indispensable.

Sitting With Koans
Essential Writings on the
Practice of Zen Koan Introspection
Edited by John Daido Loori
Foreword by Tom Kirshner
352 pages, ISBN 0-86171-369-9,
$16.95

COMING FROM WISDOM
IN JANUARY 2006

This new anthology from John Daido Loori illuminates the subtle practice of koan study from many different points of view. The book's first section includes pieces— from some of the most important scholars working in the field today—which examine the history of the study and use of koans in China and Japan. The second section includes writings from many of the most towering figures in Japanese Zen, and the final section vividly portrays the living tradition of koan introspection as it thrives today in modern times and in the West. An indispensable work for the Zen student.

About Wisdom

WISDOM PUBLICATIONS, a nonprofit publisher, is dedicated to making available authentic Buddhist works for the benefit of all. We publish translations of the sutras and tantras, commentaries and teachings of past and contemporary Buddhist masters, and original works by the world's leading Buddhist scholars. We publish our titles with the appreciation of Buddhism as a living philosophy and with the special commitment to preserve and transmit important works from all the major Buddhist traditions.

To learn more about Wisdom, or to browse books online, visit our website at wisdompubs.org. You may request a copy of our mail-order catalog online or by writing to this address:

Wisdom Publications
199 Elm Street
Somerville, Massachusetts 02144 USA
Telephone: (617) 776-7416
Fax: (617) 776-7841
Email: info@wisdompubs.org
www.wisdompubs.org

THE WISDOM TRUST

As a nonprofit publisher, Wisdom is dedicated to the publication of fine Dharma books for the benefit of all sentient beings and dependent upon the kindness and generosity of sponsors in order to do so. If you would like to make a donation to Wisdom, please do so through our Somerville office. If you would like to sponsor the publication of a book, please write or email us at the address above.

Thank you.

Wisdom is a nonprofit, charitable 501(c)(3) organization affiliated with the Foundation for the Preservation of the Mahayana Tradition (FPMT).